PELICAN BO[...]
BEYOND THE [...]
A406
RODERIC DUNKERLEY

RODERIC DUNKERLEY

BEYOND THE GOSPELS

———

PENGUIN BOOKS

Penguin Books Ltd, Harmondsworth, Middlesex
u.s.a.: Penguin Books Inc., 3300 Clipper Mill Road, Baltimore 11, Md
australia: Penguin Books Pty Ltd, 762 Whitehorse Road,
Mitcham, Victoria

—

First published 1957

—

Made and printed in Great Britain
by The Whitefriars Press Ltd
London and Tonbridge

ACKNOWLEDGEMENTS

I am grateful to John M. Watkins, London, for permission to quote passages in Ch. 5, from *The Gnostic John the Baptizer*, by G. R. S. Mead; to George Allen and Unwin Ltd, London, for permission to quote passages in Ch. 6, from Joseph Klausner's *Jesus of Nazareth*; to Harper & Brothers, New York, for permission to use passages in Ch. 10, from Dr Edgar Goodspeed's book *The Apostolic Fathers*.

I am much indebted to Professor John Foster, of Glasgow University, for reading the script of this book and for various useful suggestions he has made; also to the Rev. Patrick Rodger for his interest and care in its production.

My indebtedness to many other writers in this field of study will be apparent constantly throughout the book, and I trust that I have not anywhere overstepped the legitimate bounds of fair comment and citation. If I have done so, I will gladly make amends in any subsequent edition.

CONTENTS

CHAPTER I

INTRODUCTION – OUR QUEST

———

'THE name of Jesus is not so much written as ploughed into the history of the world,' wrote Emerson. This is a matter of fact not of faith. Opinions and convictions may differ widely as to the meaning of the fact, but the fact is beyond question.

When H. G. Wells wrote his *Outline of History* he rightly gave a prominent place to Jesus, and, when asked by a friend what half-dozen men in history deserved to be called great, the first name on his list was Jesus. And T. R. Glover, who was Lecturer in Ancient History at Cambridge, spoke of Jesus as standing at the centre of human history and said that his widespread influence is 'the most striking and outstanding fact in history. ... There is no figure in human history that signifies more.'

In illustration of this we may recall that the last 2,000 years in the West have been dominated by the movement which had its origin in him; that these centuries have been the most vital and these countries the most progressive in the history of man; that his sayings have been rendered into a thousand different languages and circulated in every corner of the globe; that no other name has ever been spoken in so many tongues, no other life-story so widely known or of such vast influence.

It is certainly no wonder then that the story of Jesus has been studied and discussed endlessly for generations and that there is a continuing search for the truth about him. Dr Glover was surely right when he said: 'Men who are to treat mankind seriously must make the intelligent effort to understand the man on whom has been centred more of the interest and passion of the most serious and the best of mankind than on any other.' We do well to try to enter more deeply into the meaning of his teaching and into the significance of his life.

Now it is of course to the four Gospels that we look for our knowledge of him – they are the source and spring of the whole matter. And the question of their trustworthiness is of vital importance. It is not possible for us to study this here – I have done so fully elsewhere. It must suffice to say that after exhaustive scientific and critical examination there is a general consensus of view amongst Christian scholars that the Gospels are adequately reliable as regards the main features of the story, though some hesitation may be felt about details. That is the basis on which the present study is made.

But there is a subsidiary question which can also claim our attention, and it is this that I propose to investigate here. It has often been neglected in spite of its intrinsic interest and certain valuable points that arise in connexion with it. It is this: What information is there about Jesus elsewhere than in the Gospels?

There is often a feeling in some people's minds that the Gospels are like prejudiced witnesses, who perhaps speak the truth but with a distinct bias. How useful it would be to have independent evidence regarding Jesus! Our task is to examine the possibility of this and to assess the value of what we find. But beyond that there is the whole question of what we may call Gospel material found outside the Gospels – that is, stories about Jesus and sayings ascribed to him elsewhere.

It is, of course, obvious that he said and did far more than the Gospels record. He was at work for two or maybe for three years, yet all the sayings given in the Gospels can be read in a few hours. We are told that 'he began to teach them many things' (Mark 6, 34), but nothing is actually quoted. And again a whole week is dismissed in a single verse (Mark 9, 2) – did he say nothing of interest during that period? It seems eminently reasonable then to suppose that many other people knew of things he had said or done which the Gospel writers either did not know, or which for some reason they did not make use of in their books. People who heard him preach would remember and repeat some of his sayings and parables; those whom he helped or healed – and also their relations and friends – must surely have talked about their wonderful experiences; and in many ways reminiscences of those golden days in Galilee must for long have been passed from one to another and from one generation to the next.

It seems strangely lacking in imagination and insight to suggest that the tradition about Jesus had become fixed and settled by the time the Gospels were written, and that there was nothing else to be learned about him outside that tradition. And in fact the author of the Fourth Gospel states quite the opposite and implies that when he wrote, probably towards the end of the first century, the known material was not exhausted in known writing. 'There are also many other things which Jesus did, the which, if they should be written every one, I suppose that even the world itself could not contain the books that should be written' (John 21, 25). Hyperbole, of course, but enshrining a real truth.

It is not surprising then when we ransack Early Christian literature that we should find here and there quite a number of sayings attributed to Jesus, and even incidents about him which the Gospels do not contain. Indeed the surprising thing really is that so few traditions have come down to us. It is not difficult to adduce reasons why many memories of him perished in early times and are now quite irrecoverable, but it would certainly have been very astonishing if the search for such extra fragments of information had been less successful than it has proved to be.

These two aspects of our study – the quest respectively for confirmatory evidence and for additional information – are of course interconnected. We cannot separate them and deal first with one and then with the other. It is our task to survey all possible sources and to glean from them whatever bears upon either side of the question.

We begin with the witness to Jesus in the New Testament elsewhere than in the Gospels. I shall not deal exhaustively with this, for it is or should be a regular part of ordinary New Testament studies. And the evidence is ready to hand in a way that most of what we have to examine is not. But it certainly demands a brief consideration in such an enquiry as this.

We then turn to non-Christian sources, both pagan and Jewish, which though not very plentiful include some interesting and significant points. The few references to Jesus in Greek and Roman writers will be considered, and in the Talmud. The evidence of Josephus, the Jewish historian, will be discussed, and in particular the puzzling question of the strange passages found in certain manuscripts of the Slavonic translation of the *Jewish War*. They have been hotly debated by scholars during the last fifty years, and if there is good reason for thinking them to be genuinely from the pen of Josephus they must be regarded as of considerable importance, since in that case they provide some valuable first-century evidence for the historicity of Jesus.

Doubts have indeed sometimes been raised as to whether Jesus did actually live at all on earth or whether the whole Christian religion is really founded upon a myth. The chief exponents of this fantastic notion were J. M. Robertson, Arthur Drews, and P. L. Couchoud, but their arguments have again and again been answered and annihilated by first-rank scholars. It is impossible even to summarize the case against them here; the point is really a subsidiary one from the main theme of the present study – it arises only because the pagan and Jewish witness to the historical Jesus is one element in the answer of Christian scholarship to the myth theorists. It must suffice to quote the words of Sir James Frazer, author of *The Golden Bough*, who has said: 'The doubts which have been cast on the historical reality of Jesus are in my judgement unworthy of serious attention.'

We come next to early Christian witness outside the New Testament, considering first some archaeological evidence from the catacombs and elsewhere. Then the works of the so-called Apostolic Fathers and those who followed closely after them in the first few centuries A.D. Here we find naturally a great many references to and quotations from the Gospels, the earliest of which provide useful confirmatory evidence of the primitive character of the Gospels – that they cannot be regarded as late documents as has sometimes been asserted. But the chief interest of these books for our purpose is that they occasionally yield additional information about Jesus and quote sayings as from him which are not found in the Gospels.

The word 'Agrapha' (pronounced 'agg-raph-ah') has been coined in modern times to denote such material; it means 'unwritten things', the suggestion being that they are found outside the official writings recognized by the Church as Gospels. They are also often called 'uncanonical sayings', and even 'apocryphal sayings', though the latter description is rather unfortunate as it appears to imply that they are not genuine – a question which is of course to be considered and not pre-judged without investigation.

Quite a number of these sayings and stories are quoted in the writings of the Church Fathers as from a Hebrew Gospel or 'Gospel according to the Hebrews'. This document is not now extant, though it is not impossible that some day it should come to light. There has been much argument as to its origin, worth, and authenticity, and the question is still undecided. But the fragments that have come down to us are certainly interesting and deserve careful study. There are also traces of a Gospel current amongst 'the Egyptians' which we shall have to notice.

The extant Apocryphal Gospels are a different matter. We must consider if they have any assistance to render us in our search, but generally speaking they are late productions of a fictitious and fanciful character. It has been thought that here or there some true recollection may have been preserved, but they are not of real importance in our study.

Another lost document to which reference will be made is Papias's *Expositions of the Sayings of the Lord*. References to it and extracts from it are found in several of the Fathers, and these are valuable as providing early evidence regarding the origin of the Gospels and other matter relevant to our quest.

Papias was probably born about A.D. 60 and claims to have had intercourse with friends of some of the disciples of Jesus. If his book should ever be discovered somewhere, as is perfectly possible, it would almost certainly add to our knowledge of all these matters and might well prove of considerable worth.

That the possibility of such books as Papias's *Expositions* and the Hebrew Gospel some day turning up is quite a real one has been shown by the discovery of the Dead Sea Scrolls. And as a matter of fact there have been unearthed amongst old rubbish heaps in Egypt many scraps of papyrus, some of which contain sayings of Jesus and a few stories not found in the Gospels. They seem to be either portions of lost Gospels or collections of traditions, and in some cases may include very primitive material. We shall pass them in review and try to assess their value. The Dead Sea Scrolls themselves are almost certainly pre-Christian, and as such lie outside the scope of our study.

Yet another possible source of extra information is to be found in the manuscripts of the canonical Gospels, where occasionally some variation occurs from the usual text or some additional words are inserted. While there are not a great many agrapha from this source, a few are of real value, and the question of their origin is an interesting one. We shall notice briefly where and how some of these manuscripts were discovered.

One group of passages remains to be considered. It may come as a surprise to those who examine this question for the first time to find that there are quite a lot of sayings ascribed to Jesus and tales told about him in Moslem writings, amongst the *Hadith* or traditions handed down from the early followers of Mohammed. What is the explanation of this odd fact? Can any of these sayings possibly be authentic? Some are at least of great interest and well worth knowing.

A few miscellaneous fragments must also be noticed, which do not fall into any of the categories mentioned, as for example some found in certain Anglo-Saxon sermons, and in a

strange book called *The Gospel of Barnabas*. And some mention must be made of one or two modern 'apocrypha', for
which claims to authenticity were quite falsely made but
which might possibly mislead the unwary.

Here then are the sources from which we are to seek to
glean evidence which will confirm what the Gospels tell
about Jesus, and at the same time to collect any further facts
regarding him which for various reasons were not included
in them. But of course we must do this in a careful and
critical manner. We are not going to accept anything at its
face value. Just as the modern mind requires us to undertake
a scientific investigation into the authenticity of the story of
Jesus in the Gospels, so it is essential that we examine these
other sources in a like manner – probing and sifting so far as
we can and gauging so far as possible the worth of what we
find. It will not be possible in a book of this size to give a full
statement of all the arguments involved in this question, but
I shall hope to give a fair summary of the position and the
usual conclusions arrived at.

One point should be noticed. When we speak of the worth
of these 'extras' we do not refer only to the genuineness or
otherwise of them as actual utterances or actions of Jesus.
There is a secondary kind of value. Even if a saying seems
probably not to have been spoken by him it may be true to
his spirit, and the fact that it was handed down by the
second or third generation of Christians may be significant.
It may preserve the impression made upon those who were
'eye-witnesses and ministers of the word'. A false anecdote
may be good history, it has been said, and a man's character
and dominating purposes may be known from the sort of
stories told about him.

This idea is of special importance, as we shall see, in the
case of the Moslem sayings to which reference has just been
made. There seems little likelihood that many of them preserve genuine recollections of Jesus, but it is not impossible
that some primitive traditions survived in the circles from
which Mohammed drew many of his first followers. In
which case, though the exact words may not be authentic,

they may embody true ideas regarding him and his teaching. They may be *ben trovati*, and well worth preserving.

Here then is our theme and something of the way in which I propose to study it. In these days when antiquarian and archaeological interests have attained some popularity a place may surely be found for these relics from the early days of our era. But, as stated at the beginning of this Introduction, they may well have real value as confirming and even extending our knowledge of Jesus Christ. Some words of Dr Rendel Harris, the eminent New Testament scholar, may be quoted in support of this idea. He argued that some of the passages which we shall deal with here 'form a collection of such importance both for his own teaching and for the knowledge of the opinions of early schools of Christian thought, that they ought certainly to be attached to the authorized scriptures in the form of an appendix.'

CHAPTER 2

OTHER NEW TESTAMENT EVIDENCE

WHILE the four Gospels are of course our principal source of information about Jesus, they are not the earliest documents which tell of him. The generally accepted dates for the composition of the Gospels as we have them are from about A.D. 65 to near the end of the first century; they may incorporate earlier writings, but these cannot be exactly identified or dated. On the other hand, Paul's letters were written, according to the usual view, between A.D. 50 and 64, and therefore antedate the Gospels, giving the oldest documentary witness to Christ.

It is not necessary to enter here into the question of the authenticity of the epistles except to say that I accept the common view that ten are genuine – excluding that is to say the three Pastorals, as they are called, addressed to Timothy and Titus, and of course Hebrews, which has no claim at all to be the work of Paul. It is true that there are probably a few personal notes of Paul's embodied in the Pastorals, but they are not material to our purpose. Doubts have also been expressed about other epistles, in particular about Ephesians, but these again do not affect our argument.

Now it is perfectly clear that to Paul Jesus was a real man and no myth. He was born 'under the law' (Gal. 4, 4), 'of the seed of David, according to the flesh' (Rom. 1, 3), his 'meekness and gentleness' were noteworthy (2 Cor. 10, 1), yet he was 'betrayed' (1 Cor. 11, 23) and 'crucified by the princes of this world' (1 Cor. 2, 8), the Jews themselves being partners in the crime (1 Thess. 2, 15), he was 'buried and rose again the third day' (1 Cor. 15, 4). One incident only of the life of Jesus is narrated at length, namely the Last Supper (1 Cor. 11, 23–5), Paul's account of which differs considerably from those in the Gospels, in particular the words 'This do, as often as ye drink it, in remembrance of me' not being found there. The corresponding words regarding the bread are thought by many scholars not to have been originally part of Luke (22, 19), but to have been brought in there from the epistle, in which case Paul supplements the Gospel narrative at this point also.

His account of the resurrection also differs greatly from those in the Gospels (1 Cor. 15, 5–8), and it is of such importance that we must notice it more closely:

> He was seen of Cephas, then of the twelve;
> After that, he was seen of above five hundred brethren at once, of whom the greater part remain unto this present, but some are fallen asleep.
> After that, he was seen of James, then of all the apostles.
> And last of all, he was seen of me also, as of one born out of due time.

This is a remarkable list of appearances both for what it leaves out and for what it includes. There is no reference to the women or the open tomb, and no statement whether the appearances took place in Jerusalem or in Galilee. We cannot be sure whether the appearance to Cephas (Peter) is one of those recorded in the Gospels (Luke 24, 34; John 21, 15–17), or whether that to the five hundred is the same as that on the mountain in Galilee (Matt. 28, 16) or on the Mount of Olives (Luke 24, 50), or whether the references are to quite different occasions. No special appearance to James is narrated in the Gospels, but there is a story in the 'Gospel according to the Hebrews' which purports to be such – we shall have to examine it in a later chapter. Finally, it is interesting to find Paul speaking of his conversion experience as one of the resurrection appearances; this raises problems as to the nature of the resurrection, but we cannot enter into that here. It is clear, then, that Paul is our earliest witness to the fact of the resurrection, but that his information about it was distinctively different from that of the Gospel writers.

Turning from the events of the life of Jesus to his teaching we find quite a number of other quotations from his words in addition to those at the Last Supper which we have just considered. For example, Paul's emphasis on love as the ful-filling of the law (Rom. 13, 10; Gal. 5, 14) is clearly remi-niscent of various passages in the Gospels. Similarly, his teaching about rendering tribute to whom it is due (Rom. 13, 7) recalls the familiar incident of the tribute money (Mark 12, 17). An interesting case is the question of the sanctity of marriage, where Paul draws a clear distinction between the commandment of the Lord and his own judge-ment on other marital problems not dealt with by Jesus (1 Cor. 7, 10–12, 25). Again, there is the teaching about the 'coming of the Lord' (1 Thess. 4, 15–17), which may be either based on Mark 13, 26, 27, or an otherwise unrecorded saying of Jesus. The number of these contacts between the epistles and the Gospels is surprising; they were gathered and studied with much diligence years ago by Canon Knowling in his book, *The Witness of the Epistles*. Sanday and Headlam, in their *Commentary on Romans*, said: 'It is very probable that much more of the common teaching and even phraseology of the Early Church than we are accustomed to imagine goes back to the teaching of Jesus.'

Possible evidence of this is found in the fact that quite a few Pauline texts are quoted in Early Christian literature as words of Jesus himself. For example, in the so-called *Apostolic Constitutions* it is stated that Jesus said at the Last Supper, 'For as often as ye eat this bread and drink this cup ye do shew my death till I come.' It is not clear from 1 Cor. 11, 26 whether this sentence is intended as part of what Jesus said or whether it is a comment by the apostle. Again, in 1 Cor. 11, 18, 19, we read of 'schisms' and 'factions' in the Church (see R.V. margin), and in Justin Martyr's *Dialogue* he quotes Jesus as saying 'There shall be schisms and fac-tions.' Once more, in an ancient book ascribed to Cyprian, called *Concerning Gamblers*, we find the saying attributed to Jesus, 'Grieve not the Holy Spirit which is in you, and quench not the light which has shone in you', and two texts of Paul's look extremely like references to such a saying

(Eph. 4, 30 – 'Grieve not the Holy Spirit of God', and 1
Thess. 5, 19 – 'Quench not the Spirit').

Surprise has sometimes been felt that there is not more
about the life and teaching of Jesus in the epistles, but the
facts already advanced suggest that Paul's knowledge of
Jesus was by no means as scanty as has sometimes been
thought. And when we consider presently the evidence of
Acts we shall find confirmation of this view. But two points
must always be borne in mind. While Paul's faith was
deeply rooted in the historic facts of the Gospel, yet his main
interest was naturally in the living Christ with whom he
companied. Whether he had ever met Jesus in the flesh we
cannot know for certain, but that mattered less to him than
the fact that he knew him in the Spirit. Moreover, the
epistles were not formal declarations of faith requiring full
and balanced testimony regarding the beginnings of the
Christian movement; they were occasional documents hur-
riedly written to meet emergencies or deal with particular
situations. The need for much reference to the ministry of
Jesus did not arise.

Leaving now the epistles of Paul we must look next at
Acts. And first, what has been said about Paul's knowledge
of Jesus must be supplemented by what he is stated to have
said. This cannot be deemed to be quite as valuable evidence as that from the epistles, for it is second-hand – re-
ports about Paul written towards the end of the first century.
Nevertheless it is of real value. We notice several references
to him preaching 'the kingdom of God' (14, 22; 20, 25;
19, 8; 28, 23, 31), and there is the remarkable statement of
his critics at Thessalonica that he was affirming that there
was 'another king, one Jesus' (17, 7). It often used to be
said that Paul's emphasis was on the Church and not on the
kingdom as in the case of Jesus, but this is clearly an exaggeration. In the epistles he has to speak much of the Church
because of the practical problems that had arisen with which
he had to deal, but probably his ordinary preaching was
more akin to the Gospels than has often been thought. We
may remember too that there are quite a number of state-

ments in the epistles about the kingdom which show that it was a live topic in his mind (Rom. 14, 17; 1 Cor. 4, 20; 6, 9, 10; 15, 20; Gal. 5, 21).

We examine next Paul's speeches, in particular the sermon at Antioch (13, 16 f.) and his farewell talk with the Ephesian elders at Miletus (20, 18–35). For our purpose we may ignore the shorter addresses at Lystra and Athens (14, 15–17, and 17, 22–31), and also his several defences (chaps. 22, 24, 26). How far the accounts in Acts of what Paul said are genuine and authentic is an open question; it is common to regard them as similar to speeches quoted in Greek and Roman histories which are usually thought to be the fabrications of the writers, but I feel very doubtful about this so far as Acts is concerned. If, as I hold, the book was the work of Luke, the travelling companion of Paul, it seems reasonable to suppose that, while not verbatim records, the gist at least of what was said has been preserved.

In the sermon at Antioch we find references to the Davidic descent of Jesus, to the baptism of John and his promise of the One coming after him, to the people and rulers at Jerusalem rejecting Jesus and demanding his death from Pilate, to his burial and resurrection. The quotations from Old Testament prophecy are not material to our purpose, which is simply to show the extent of Paul's probable knowledge of the Gospel facts. This really confirms and expands the evidence from the epistles. The other passage, from Miletus, is of even greater interest because of its reminiscences of the teaching of Jesus. There is the description of the Church as a flock (Acts 20, 28, 29 – cf. Luke 12, 32; Matt. 7, 15) and of the wolves attacking it; there is the warning word 'watch', which reminds us of the Gethsemane story and other passages (v. 31 – cf. Mark 13, 35; 14, 38); and more particularly there is the beautiful saying in verse 35, which is full of the spirit of the Sermon on the Mount and might well have been included there, 'It is more blessed to give than to receive.' But it is not only this actual saying that is valuable here; the way it is introduced makes it clear that it was part of the well-known 'words of Jesus' and that

Paul was bidding them remember and obey such teaching.

Apart from the witness of Paul, we have in Acts the Ascension story and words of Jesus (1, 4–10) more fully than in the Gospels, Peter's speeches at Pentecost and subsequently, in which the crucifixion and resurrection are repeatedly declared, and Stephen's address before his death. There is no need to give full references or to discuss in detail. We may just notice that Peter's précis of the Gospel story (10, 36–41) looks very like Mark's Gospel in miniature, and may indeed represent the first draft of the evangelic narrative. 'Who went about doing good, and healing all that were oppressed of the devil, for God was with him' – is a masterly summing-up of the Galilean ministry. Other points to notice from the several speeches are the title 'the Prince of life' (3, 15 – cf. John 10, 10, etc.), the denunciation of the crucifixion as murder (7, 52), and the twofold statement that Jesus himself said, 'John truly baptized with water, but ye shall be baptized with the Holy Ghost' (1, 5; 11, 16) – a promise which in the Gospels is made by John, not by Jesus (Mark 1, 8, etc.).

There is very little of moment, so far as we are concerned here, in the rest of the New Testament. There are many references to the death and sufferings of Jesus, but few to his life and teaching. In Hebrews we read twice of his being tempted (2, 18; 4, 15), and of his enduring the 'contradiction of sinners against himself' (12, 3). In 1 Peter we have one clear reference to the teaching of Jesus – 'that they may by your good works which they shall behold glorify God in the day of visitation' (2, 12 – cf. Matt. 5, 16); and a striking picture of the passion of Christ – 'who when he was reviled reviled not again, when he suffered he threatened not, but committed himself to him that judgeth righteously' (2, 23). The mention of the Transfiguration in 2 Peter 1, 17, 18, cannot be deemed of much value, as the book is almost certainly late and of unknown authorship, and there is no likelihood that this reference is independent of the Gospel account.

One final point is of considerable interest. The Epistle of

James was dubbed by Martin Luther 'an epistle of straw' because of its lack of theological teaching. Its emphasis is ethical and practical, and it has often been thought that it contains recollections of sayings of Jesus not recorded in the Gospels. A few of these may be mentioned:

Blessed is the man that endureth temptation, for when he is tried he shall receive the crown of life, which the Lord hath promised to them that love him (1, 12).

Be ye doers of the word and not hearers only, deceiving your own selves (1, 22).

Doth a fountain send forth at the same place sweet water and bitter? Can the fig tree bear olive berries, either a vine figs? So can no fountain both yield salt water and fresh (3, 11, 12).

Know ye not that the friendship of the world is enmity with God? Whosoever therefore will be the friend of the world is the enemy of God (4, 4).

Dr J. H. Moulton spoke of the writer of this epistle being saturated in the ideas of the Sermon on the Mount – 'his short passages are simply studded with quotations from or allusions to the words of Jesus', while another writer said that the epistle tells little about Jesus (there are only two mentions of his name) simply because it is almost made up of his words. We certainly feel much more in the atmosphere of the Gospels than in any of the other epistles. This has been well demonstrated by L. E. Elliott-Binns in his recent little book *Galilean Christianity* (pp. 45 f.).

To sum up: we have in the New Testament outside the Gospels ample confirmatory evidence regarding the main facts of the Gospel story, the nature and spirit of the teaching of Jesus, his character and the supreme worth of it to mankind. Some small points of additional information have been gleaned also, and there is clear evidence that in early days more was known of what he said and did than found its way into the four Gospels. We are therefore encouraged to go forward in our quest.

CHAPTER 3

PAGAN EVIDENCE

THERE is very little witness to Jesus in non-Christian writers during the first hundred years after the crucifixion. Harnack, the famous Church historian, once said that it could all be written down on a single sheet of paper. We will consider presently the reasons why it is so scanty and whether the fact is of much importance. But let us first pass in review what references there are.

The earliest is found in the letter which Pliny wrote to the Emperor Trajan in A.D. 110 from Bithynia, where he was serving as pro-consul. He asked for instructions as to how to deal with Christians, of whom there were a great number in the province, so much so that the temples had been almost abandoned. He regarded Christianity as a base and degrading superstition 'carried to great lengths', and had taken certain steps to counteract its influence which were in part successful. He tells of some who when called upon to do so 'reverenced your statue and the images of the gods, and reviled Christ.' He speaks of torturing two women 'called deaconesses', and of there being a marked revival of pagan worship as a result of the measures he had taken. He gives a slight glimpse of the Christians meeting 'on a particular day before dawn and singing a hymn to Christ as though to a god.' And he says that they bound themselves by an oath to abstain from crime and to behave honestly. After this the assembly broke up, but met again in the evening to partake of a common meal. This information about the worship of the Early Church is of great interest, but from our point of view it is unfortunate that the reference to Christ himself is so meagre. In his reply Trajan commended Pliny's actions 'in investigating the cases of those who have been denounced to you as Christians', but said that they were not to be sought out. 'If denounced and proved to be Christians, they must be punished, with the proviso however that everyone who denies that he is a Christian and proves his assertion by acts, that is by supplicating our gods, should though open to suspicion in the past gain pardon by his repentance.'

Our next witness is the Roman historian Tacitus, writing about the year 115. Referring to Nero's persecution of Christians in 64 he says, 'This name comes to them from Christ, who was executed in the reign of Tiberius by the procurator Pontius Pilate, and the detestable superstition, suppressed for a time, broke out again and spread not only over Judea, where this evil originated, but even throughout Rome, where everything on earth that is vile finds its way and is practised.' A terrible description of the persecution follows. There is another but slighter reference elsewhere in Tacitus to the Christians 'having been convicted of a hatred of the human race', but Christ himself is not mentioned. Doubts concerning the authenticity of Tacitus's extant works were raised late in the nineteenth century by a French historian named Hochart, who thought that they had been forged by an Italian writer, Poggio Bracciolini, in the fifteenth century. These doubts if substantiated would of course have invalidated Tacitus's witness to Christ, but Hochart gained practically no support for his views. Various references and minute details in the disputed books have been proved to correspond closely with the evidence of inscriptions and coins discovered since Bracciolini's time.

We come now to Suetonius, writing about 120. In his *Life of Claudius*, who was emperor from 41 to 54, he says that 'he expelled from Rome the Jews, who under the influence of Chrestus made great tumult.' This is commonly assumed to be the expulsion of Jews mentioned in Acts 18, 2, when Aquila and Priscilla came from the city to Corinth, where they met St Paul, the date being about 52. If this is so, it constitutes an interesting link between Christian and Roman documents of very early date. It cannot of course be proved that the 'Chrestus' referred to by Suetonius was indeed Jesus Christ – the names having been confused as frequently happened, and the writer thinking mistakenly that the leader whose name he had heard in connexion with the riots was actually himself present there and then. But it is generally thought that the identification is reasonably certain, and that such a confusion is just what might be expected in information based upon hearsay. That disturbances were taking place in Rome at such an early date, long before Paul arrived, is of course remarkable, but his letter to the Romans shows the early growth of the Church there. There were Roman Jews in Jerusalem at Pentecost (Acts 2, 10), and those who were gathered into the Church then would naturally return home and take with them the astonishing news that the Christ was believed to have appeared in Palestine and to have been killed in Jerusalem. Such tidings would inevitably arouse strong feelings and much opposition, as it always did when Paul proclaimed these things. In addition to this passage there is also a brief reference in Suetonius's *Life of Nero* to the effect that 'the Christians, a set of men of a new and mischievous superstition, were punished.' This is valuable confirmation of the fact of the Neronian persecution, but there is no actual mention of Jesus himself.

These are the three principal witnesses from the pagan world in the earliest times to the historicity of Jesus; they do not tell us much about him, but it is clear that these writers knew of his existence and of the spread of the movement which originated from him. There is no suggestion that he was a mythical character. They place him definitely in his historical context and make havoc of the fantastic theories that he never lived.

Two letters of the Emperor Hadrian, who succeeded Trajan and ruled from 117 to 138, may also be noticed. One, preserved by the Church historian Eusebius, was written to Minucius Fundanus, proconsul of Asia in 125, ordering that the Christians should not be put to death without a formal accusation and a proper hearing of their case. The reason for Hadrian so writing has been thought to have been an apology addressed to him by Quadratus, a Christian philosopher of Athens, to which we shall refer in a later chapter. The other letter, preserved by Vopiscus in his *Life of Saturninus*, was sent to the consul Servianus in 134; in it Hadrian speaks scornfully of the mixture of religions in Egypt, thus:

> Those who worship Serapis are likewise Christians; even those who style themselves the bishops of Christ are devoted to Serapis. The very patriarch is forced by some to adore Serapis, by others to worship Christ. There is but one God for them all. Him do the Christians, him do the Jews, him do the Gentiles all alike worship.

This is perplexing, of course, but the only point that concerns us at the moment is Hadrian's familiarity with the name of Christ. The genuineness of both these letters has been disputed, but Lightfoot argued strongly for the second, and Foakes-Jackson in his *History of the Christian Church* accepts them both.

Another point of interest is that in Cureton's *Spicilegium Syriacum* there is a Syriac letter of a certain Mara bar Serapion, who fled from Samosata when it was seized by Vespasian in 73 and probably wrote not long after; in the course of the letter he says, 'Or what profit had the Jews from the execution of their wise king, seeing that from that time forward the kingdom was taken away from them?' C. H. Dodd speaks of this as probably dating from early in the second century, but in any case it seems an interesting and useful piece of confirmatory evidence both of the fact of Christ and of the early spread of knowledge of him.

There are also some secondary witnesses whom we should notice – writers, that is to say, whose books have not survived but whose statements come to us at second-hand through Christian writers quoting them. Origen (*c.* 250), one of the greatest scholars of the Early Church, states that Phlegon (*c.* 80–140), a freedman of the Emperor Hadrian, spoke in one of his historical works of the founder of the Christian faith making certain predictions which had come to pass. And Julius Africanus (221) says, 'Thallus, in the third book of his history, calls this darkness (i.e. at the crucifixion) an eclipse of the sun, but in my opinion he is wrong.' This seems to mean that Thallus knew the Christian tradition about the darkness but interpreted it as due to natural causes. Who was this Thallus and when did he write? Eusebius says that Thallus wrote a history in three books, and Josephus states that a Samaritan so named lent a large sum of money to Agrippa shortly before the latter became king of Judea in 41. If this is the same man and if he wrote somewhere in the middle of the first century, we have here some very early witness to the tradition of the crucifixion. But the link seems a slender one on which little reliance can be placed.

Pagan attacks on Christianity in the second and third centuries were answered by various apologists, to some of whose works we shall refer in a later chapter. Meanwhile we will notice a few of the criticisms that were made – again as items of historical evidence of the writers' acquaintance with the fact of Christ and the expansion of the Church.

Lucian, the satirist, in the reign of Marcus Aurelius (161–180), refers to the 'crucified sophist' and ridicules Christians as ignorant and credulous people, liable to be deluded by any clever charlatan. A tutor of the Emperor named Fronto lent his name to libellous charges against the Christians, asserting that they engaged in shameful orgies at their love feasts. Numenius (170) is stated by Origen to have 'set forth a narrative about Jesus without naming him.' The greatest of these opponents of the Church was Celsus (178), whose attack on Christianity was exhaustively dealt with by Origen. He had a fairly extensive knowledge of the facts of the Gospel and argued vigorously about the Virgin Birth, miracles, the Resurrection, and so forth. Some of his statements are of an apocryphal nature – that Jesus was born out of wedlock (the Jewish libel found, as we shall see, in the Talmud), that he was 'little, ill-favoured, and ignoble', that because of poverty he went to Egypt and worked as a hired labourer, learning magic while there, that he went about begging and gathered round him ten or twelve infamous men.

An interesting little book containing some of the material

dealt with in this chapter is Haines's *Heathen Contacts with Christianity during its First Century and a Half* (1923). A fuller study of the conflict with paganism will be found in Professor John Foster's *After the Apostles* (1951), to which I am indebted especially as regards Celsus.

One other point may be mentioned. In 1856 a crude caricature of the crucifixion was found scratched on the wall of an ancient building at Rome. It shows a man's body with an ass's head hanging on a cross, the outstretched arms fastened to the cross-beam. At the side stands a figure of a boy with hand upraised as though in adoration. Underneath in rough careless writing are the words –

Alexamenos worships his god.

The date of this graffito is at the end of the second or the beginning of the third century, and it is of particular interest because several apologists of the second century refer to anti-Christian mockery of this sort. Tertullian, for example, says, 'Like some others, you are under the delusion that our god is an ass's head. ... You think we render superstitious adoration to the cross.' And the heathen opponent of Minucius Felix is represented as saying, 'I hear the Christians adore the head of an ass ... and explain their ceremonies by reference to a man punished on a cross.' Foster reproduces this graffito on the cover of his book which has just been mentioned.

It may be repeated, for the point is of considerable importance, that in none of these various testimonies to the fact of Christ is there any slightest hint or idea that he was not a real historical person. We shall see exactly the same thing in a later chapter when we consider the Jewish references to him in the Talmud – whatever opposition or criticism is levelled at him and at the Church, his historicity is taken for granted. Indeed it has been argued – and I think very rightly – that myth theories of the beginnings of Christianity are modern speculative hypotheses motivated by unreasoning prejudice and dislike. 'It would never enter anyone's head,' says Merezhkovsky, 'to ask whether Jesus had lived, unless before asking the question the mind had been darkened by the wish that he had not lived.'

We come now to the question why there are so few witnesses at first from pagan sources and why their evidence is so meagre. The answer is, to begin with, that there is comparatively little literature of any kind dating from the first century after Christ. It is difficult for us in these days of quick and full records, and of complete and documented histories, to think back into ancient conditions and to realize how slender are our links with the distant past. For example, our chief authority for some of the history of the Roman Empire is Tacitus, who wrote thirty books. Of these only thirteen remain in full, with fragments of four others, all in manuscripts of late date, while some parts are found in one manuscript only, and that of the tenth century. When our witnesses to events of general history are so few and fragmentary, it is surely no wonder that there are such scanty references to Christ.

But secondly it must be remembered that at first the significance and importance of the life and death of Jesus were not apparent, and therefore there was no occasion for secular writers to mention him. 'To the official world,' it has been said, 'the execution of a carpenter of Nazareth was the most insignificant event of Roman history during those decades. It disappeared completely among the innumerable executions inflicted by the Roman provincial administration. It would be a most miraculous accident had it been mentioned in any official report.' We may recall Anatole France's well-known story of Pilate as an old man being asked if he remembered the trial and death of Jesus, and how he could not recall it at all. This point has been combated by Dr Robert Eisler, in his massive work *The Messiah Jesus*, to which we shall have occasion to refer in a later chapter. He contends that political issues were involved in the death of Jesus, which must have been fully reported at Rome, and that records of the trial must have been lodged in the Imperial archives.

We cannot speak confidently therefore about this. But

Eisler offers another explanation of the scarcity of pagan references to Jesus, and there may be some substance in it. He maintains that from the time of Constantine (312) the Church possessed state authority to suppress all anti-Christian literature. This was done both by destroying pagan and Jewish books wholesale, and by censoring them; he gives photographs of manuscripts, and later of printed books with lines and paragraphs obliterated. He thinks that there can be no doubt that there were many more statements about Jesus in ancient times which have not survived because they were regarded as blasphemous by the Christian authorities.

There we must leave the matter. Enough has, I think, been said to show that, while the pagan witness to Jesus in the first hundred years after his death is not considerable, yet neither is it negligible, and that there are a number of possible reasons why it is not greater than it is.

CHAPTER 4

THE WITNESS OF JOSEPHUS

JOSEPHUS, the Jewish historian, was born in Jerusalem A.D. 37–8, and died about the end of the century. He was therefore a younger contemporary of St Paul and must have been well aware of the rise of the Christian Church. He took part in the revolt of the Jews against Rome, but later deserted to the enemy and became an associate of the Emperor Vespasian and his son Titus at the siege and fall of Jerusalem.

His two most important works are the *Jewish War*, written between 70 and 75, and his *Jewish Antiquities*, some twenty years later. It seems natural to expect that these books should contain some notice of the Christian movement and some references to its Founder. It has always been a puzzle to scholars that they contain so little material of this kind and that what they have is of such uncertain value. The first two books of the *War* describe the circumstances that led up to the conflict, and the 'silence of Josephus' about Jesus and the Church seems very strange; in the ordinary Greek version there are no references of any kind.

In the *Antiquities* there are three passages to be considered. The first deals with John the Baptist, not with Jesus, but it is of importance as linking the Gospel story with secular history. It is commonly accepted as genuine, and though the reason given for John's arrest is different from that in the Gospels it is not really inconsistent with it – both motives may easily have operated to determine Herod's action.

Some of the Jews, however, regarded the destruction of Herod's army as the work of God, who thus exacted very righteous retribution for John surnamed the Baptist. For Herod had slain John – a good man who bade the Jews to cultivate virtue by justice towards each other and piety towards God, and to come to baptism; for

immersion, he said, would only appear acceptable to God if practised, not as an expiation for specific offences, but for the purification of the body, when the soul had been thoroughly cleansed by
righteousness. Now when men flocked to him – for they were
highly elated at listening to his words – Herod feared that the
powerful influence which he exercised over men's minds might
lead to some form of revolt, for they seemed ready to do anything
on his advice. To forestall and kill him seemed better than a be-
lated repentance when plunged in the turmoil of an insurrection.
And so, through Herod's suspicions, John was sent as a prisoner to
the fortress of Machaerus and there put to death. The Jews therefore thought that the destruction of Herod's army was the penalty
deliberately inflicted upon him by God to avenge John.

The second passage is more controversial, and at the same
time, if it is actually from the pen of Josephus himself, much
more interesting and valuable. It is found in all extant
manuscripts of the *Antiquities*, and from the time of Eusebius
in the fourth century, who quoted it in his *Church History*,
down to comparatively modern times its genuineness was
not doubted. It was largely because of it that Whiston's
Josephus was often found a few generations ago in Christian
homes alongside the Bible. Here it is:

Now about this time arose Jesus, a wise man, if indeed he should
be called a man. For he was a doer of marvellous deeds, a teacher
of men who receive the truth with pleasure; and he won over to
himself many Jews and many also of the Greek (nation). He was
the Christ. And when on the indictment of the principal men
among us Pilate had sentenced him to the cross those who had
loved him at the first did not cease; for he appeared to them on the
third day alive again, the divine prophets having foretold these and
ten thousand other wonderful things concerning him. And even
now the tribe of Christians named after him is not extinct.

When the age of criticism dawned, strong arguments were
soon levelled against the authenticity of this passage both on
external and on internal grounds. On the one hand, the absence of any earlier reference than that of Eusebius was
stressed – and, more particularly, Origen, a hundred years
earlier than Eusebius, not only does not quote it but twice
remarks that Josephus did not believe in Jesus as Christ. On

the other, the words 'He was the Christ' and the reference to the resurrection would seem to imply that the writer was a Christian, which Josephus certainly was not.

As a result of such arguments it came to be generally held that the passage was not the work of Josephus. Various explanations of it were advanced, but no general agreement was reached. Sometimes it was thought that it was wholly a Christian forgery – perhaps inserted in place of an uncomplimentary statement about Jesus which piety had excised. Sometimes it was held that the basis of the passage was by Josephus, but that various words had been interpolated or altered. The most recent theory of this kind is that of Dr Robert Eisler in *The Messiah Jesus*, to which reference is made below, but his hypothetical reconstruction is of a highly speculative character and has not won much support.

There have been, however, strong supporters of the opposite view that the passage is substantially genuine. Dr F. C. Burkitt urged this idea and won the assent of Harnack. It is maintained that the passage is really 'a masterpiece of non-committal statement' rather than an acknowledgement of anything like faith in Christ, and that it is difficult to think of a Christian penning it. The phrase of greatest significance – 'He was the Christ' – may be regarded as merely a historical explanation that the man referred to was the founder of the Christian sect, of whom the readers of the book had doubtless heard. Just as if a modern writer mentioned Gandhi and added – 'I mean the Mahatma' – without intending to suggest that he himself accepted the idea involved in that word.

The third passage in the *Antiquities* which concerns us is very slight. It occurs in a story of the martyrdom of James, the brother of Jesus, who was (as we know from Acts) one of the leaders of the Jerusalem Church:

(Ananus) assembled the sanhedrim of the judges, and brought before them the brother of Jesus, who was called Christ, whose name was James, and some others, and when he had formed an accusation against them as breakers of the law, he delivered them to be stoned.

There is no evidence at all that this phrase 'who was called Christ' should be considered a Christian addition, and if the previously quoted passage is genuine it would seem entirely natural that such a reference back to it should be found here, while if it should not be so this one stands on its own as a witness to Josephus's acquaintance with the fact of Christ. Not only so, but it reveals his knowledge of the Christian movement, the stoning of James being confirmed by other evidence.

The sum of the matter as regards the *Antiquities* seems to be, then, that there is quite a reasonable case for thinking that Josephus was aware of the facts about Jesus and the rise of the Church. And while no fresh information has come to us from this book, it is of considerable importance that we may have in this way first-century testimony to Jesus from beyond the Gospels.

When we turn to the *Jewish War* the case is very different. As already stated, there are no references to Jesus or the Church in the familiar Greek version. There are various possible explanations of this 'silence'. Josephus may have deliberately avoided any mention of Jesus for reasons that seemed good to him. If he showed an appreciation of John in the passage in the *Antiquities* it would not appear unlikely that he felt in somewhat the same way about Jesus, but he may easily have felt it impolitic to say so publicly. His fellow Jews might resent any hint of approval, while his Roman readers might object to any suggestion that a good man had been crucified by their procurator. He may therefore have 'resorted to a cowardly silence' for some such reason.

But of course it may not have been an actual silence at all. There may have been a passage or passages in his original script and in early copies of it which were omitted in later copies for reasons similar to those just mentioned. All extant manuscripts of the *War* date from the tenth or eleventh century, and it is obviously impossible to feel certain that we have the text as it left his hands. Now it is an interesting fact that in the Old Russian or Slavonic version of the *War* there are a number of passages regarding John, Jesus, and the Church. And the question of course arises whether they are late Christian interpolations or whether in some mysterious way they come from the original script of Josephus.

It is known that some years before he wrote in Greek (with the help of Greek literary assistants owing to his elementary knowledge of Greek) he had written an earlier draft of the *War* in his native Aramaic for the use of those whom he calls the Upper Barbarians – Parthians and Babylonians, and especially the Jews living among them. His purpose in so writing was to deter them from revolting against the Romans and so experiencing the disasters and miseries that had come upon the Jews in Palestine. He might clearly include material in such a document which later on he would exclude from the more polished work which was intended for the Emperor and his associates.

The earliest study of these Slavonic passages was made by Berendts (1906), who thought that they were indeed substantially from this Aramaic draft, though no doubt containing later interpolations. Most scholars rejected this idea and considered them very late additions and quite worthless, but others felt less sure. Seeberg and Frey thought that, though not the work of Josephus himself, they were based on early oral information and 'worthy of attention as giving a picture of an early outside view of nascent Christianity.' The first English translation and study of them was made by G. R. S. Mead in *The Quest*, and subsequently in book form (1924), whose opinion was that they were developed from echoes of popular traditions still floating about in the Jewish environment of Christianity towards the end of the first century.

These views did not win much support, and it was generally held that these passages were late Christian interpolations containing no primitive material. Then in 1928 Dr Robert Eisler's monumental work on the question appeared, a somewhat abbreviated English edition being published in 1931 under the title *The Messiah Jesus*. His first view was that the Slavonic *War* was translated direct from the Aramaic draft already referred to, but he presently modified this idea because it was shown that there were many indications that it was translated from a Greek text. He suggested that Josephus's first rough draft in Aramaic was rendered into Greek by his assistants, but that it had a very limited circulation, and that it was from this that the Slavonic version was made. He believed that some copy or copies of this early Greek edition were preserved in some Jewish library, from which they were taken and translated into Slavonic in the fifteenth century, from which period the extant manuscripts of the Slavonic *War* date. It is known that at this time there was a Judaizing sect in Russia with which the Orthodox Church had to contend, and Eisler maintained that this version was part of their anti-Christian propaganda.

On the basis of these passages and certain other apocryphal material Eisler worked out an extraordinary theory of Jesus adopting a political messiahship and becoming involved in an armed clash with Rome. He made great play with the reference in Mark 15, 7 to '*the* insurrection' and to the fact that the disciples carried swords. He believed that several hundreds gathered armed on the Mount of Olives and marched with Jesus riding at their head into the city. The Roman cohort was too small to take effective action and help had to be sought from the garrison at Caesarea. For some days the Temple was occupied, but presently the inevitable happened and the movement was suppressed. The Galileans whose blood Pilate mingled with their sacrifices (Luke 13, 1) were the armed followers of Jesus.

Many critical reviews of Eisler's work appeared. His use of the documents in question was generally felt to be so arbitrary and uncritical that his theory based upon them was utterly discredited. One writer spoke of it as a 'cascade d'hypothèses imaginées'. A valuable study of the whole matter was contributed to the *Harvard Theological Review* (1932) by Professor J. M. Creed, while a long and learned book by Dr J. W. Jack entitled *The Historic Christ* (1933) – a careful

examination of the Slavonic Josephus and of Eisler's theory
– was felt by most scholars to have finally disposed of this
strange chapter of New Testament study.

In contrast to Eisler's explanation of the Slavonic passages as primitive Josephus material used in anti-Christian
propaganda, Jack and Creed thought they were part of the
Orthodox counterblast to the Judaizing heresy to which
reference has been made. There are difficulties about this,
however, because their propaganda value does not appear
to be very great – a Christian apologist who produced them
might well be deemed not to have known his job. Indeed
there are other fully Christian passages in these Slavonic
manuscripts (which are obvious interpolations); why then
are these of such an unconvincing and ineffective character?
Some scholars have therefore agreed with Eisler in thinking
them of Jewish origin for anti-Christian propaganda though
disagreeing about them coming from Josephus or being of
early date, believing rather that they were invented as well
as interpolated in the fifteenth century. But again this does
not appear very likely; would such antagonists of the Church
have been content with such vague and non-committal
statements?

The riddle of the passages can therefore hardly be said to
have been solved. And recently it has been re-opened by Dr
S. G. F. Brandon in his book *The Fall of Jerusalem* (1951).
He believes it is not impossible that the Slavonic *War* may
preserve Josephus's original writing. He recognizes the ex-
travagances of Eisler's work, but thinks that there probably
was a stronger political element in primitive Christianity
and that the Church was more closely associated with the
cause of Jewish nationalism than has been generally supposed. Now, I consider it to be very significant that such a
scholar as Dr Brandon does not feel that a conclusive case
has been made out against the authenticity of these passages. One has often wondered what an outsider, a non-
Christian Jew of the first century in Palestine, would have
known and thought about Jesus. And it is most intriguing to
feel that we may have in the Slavonic Josephus a genuine

work of that import dating from a few decades after the crucifixion.

This does not of course mean that any great reliance can be placed upon these passages in detail. There is far more reason for accepting the general trustworthiness of the Gospels than for assessing Josephus or someone else writing in his name as a first-class witness. But they may have this one positive contribution to make to our thought – that the political implications of the Gospel were more fully recognized in early Christian times than has often been supposed. It has very commonly been assumed and taught that the Gospel was – and was regarded in the Early Church as – a purely subjective and spiritual affair. Apart from anything else, the *Magnificat* should have shown that to be an error (Luke 2, 52: 'He hath put down the mighty from their seats, and exalted them of low degree') – there was obviously a potential threat to the established order of things in the coming of Christ. And it was clearly implicit in the preaching of the kingdom of God that sooner or later political issues would become involved; the story of Paul at Thessalonica is sufficient witness to that (Acts 17, 6, 7) – 'these that have turned the world upside down have come hither also ... saying that there is another king, one Jesus.' That is revolution, but by truth and grace not by armed force.

It comes then to this – that there is a possibility but nothing like certainty that we have in these Slavonic passages some first-century witness to the historicity of Jesus and to the start of the Christian Church. They may even have come from Josephus himself. If either of these possibilities is correct, it is a matter of considerable interest and importance, since non-Christian evidence from those days is so scanty. They may perhaps preserve a vague memory of certain political repercussions to the preaching of the Gospel, some of the followers of Jesus then having marred his intention as many have done in later times by substituting subversive and coercive measures for peace and goodwill. But much uncertainty must at present remain concerning them. At the best they give us just the garbled second-hand, half-correct version of events that we might have expected under the circumstances, based upon rumours and hearsay and untrustworthy gossip.

A fuller study of this whole question will be found in the article which I contributed to the *Hibbert Journal* (January 1955). As these passages are not easily available in English, I have decided to print them in the following chapter, making use of the translation of G. R. S. Mead.*

* See his *The Gnostic John the Baptizer*, by kind permission of the publisher, John M. Watkins.

CHAPTER 5

THE SLAVONIC PASSAGES

====

THERE are eight of these passages, the longest (IV) being that which deals with the life of Jesus; we will quote it in full. Two of the others (VI and VIII) are brief but interesting; the remaining five refer to John the Baptist, the Early Church, and portents at the death of Jesus – these I have had to abbreviate somewhat.

(I) Now at that time a man went about among the Jews in strange garments, for he had put pelts on his body everywhere where it was not covered with his own hair. Indeed to look at he was like a wild man.

He came to the Jews and summoned them to freedom, saying, God hath sent me, that I may show you the way of the law wherein ye may free yourselves from many holders of power. And there will be no mortal ruling over you, only the Highest who hath sent me. And when the people heard this, they were joyful. And there went after him all Judea, that lies in the region round about Jerusalem.

And he did nothing else to them save that he plunged them into the stream of the Jordan and dismissed them, instructing them that they should cease from evil works, and promising that there would then be given them a ruler who would set them free and subject to them all that is not in submission. But no one of whom we speak would himself be subjected. Some reviled but others got faith.

And when he had been brought to Archelaus and the doctors of the law had assembled, they asked him who he is and where he has been until then. And to this he made answer and spake, I am pure; the Spirit of God hath led me on, and I live on cane and roots and tree-food. But when they threatened to put him to torture if he would not cease from those words and deeds, he nevertheless said, It is meet for you rather to cease from your heinous works and cleave unto the Lord your God.

And there rose up in anger Simon an Essene by extraction, a scribe, and he spake, We read every day the divine books. But thou

41

only now come from the forest like a wild animal – thou darest in
sooth to teach us and to mislead the people with thy reprobate
words. And he rushed forward to do him bodily violence. But he
rebuking them spake, I will not disclose to you the mystery which
dwelleth in you, for ye have not desired it. Thereby an untold
calamity is come upon you, and because of yourselves.

And when he had thus spoken, he went forth to the other side of
the Jordan, and while no one durst rebuke him, that one did what
he had done also heretofore.

This passage follows an account in the ordinary version
of the *Jewish War* regarding the reign of Archelaus, the son
of Herod the Great (Matt. 2, 22). But he was banished by
the Emperor in A.D. 6, so that the reference to him here as
examining John is an anachronism which it seems exceedingly unlikely a Christian forger would perpetrate with the
Gospels in front of him, where John first appears on the
scene in 29 (Luke 3, 1). It is much more likely that the
writer was misinformed as to the date of John's preaching
and inserted the story here without good reason. The absence of the name of John here should be noticed – and
similarly the fact that the name Jesus does not occur in passage III.

(II) The second passage need not detain us; it tells of a
dream of Herod Philip, which 'that man of whom we have
previously written' interpreted, and of Philip's subsequent
death. It pictures the character of Philip in an unfavourable
light, which is in contrast to a passage in the *Antiquities*,
where he is praised for his mild disposition. The next passage
follows immediately.

(III) And Herod his brother took his wife Herodias. And because
of her all the doctors of the Law abhorred him, but durst not accuse
him before his face. But only that one whom they called a wild man
came to him in anger and spake, Why hast thou taken the wife of
thy brother? As thy brother hath died a death void of pity, thou
too wilt be reaped off by the heavenly sickle. God's decree will not
be silenced, but will destroy thee through evil affliction in foreign
lands. For thou dost not raise up seed for thy brother, but grati-

fiest thy fleshly lust and committest adultery, seeing that four children of him are alive.

Now when Herod heard this he was filled with wrath and commanded that they should beat him and drive him away. But he accused Herod incessantly wherever he found him, and right up to the time when he put him under arrest and gave orders to slay him.

Now his disposition was extraordinary and his mode of life not that of a man; indeed just like a bodiless spirit, thus did this one too continue. His lips knew no bread; not even at the Passover did he taste unleavened bread, saying that in remembrance of God who had freed the people from slavery it was given for eating in the flight, for the way was in haste. To wine and intoxicating drink he let himself not even draw near. And every animal he abhorred, and every wrong he rebuked, and tree-produce served him for use.

While this agrees with the canonical account that the arrest of John was due to his condemnation of Herod's adultery with Herodias – which is quite different from the statement in the *Antiquities*, as we saw in the last chapter – yet the details are not at all the same. Here Philip is already dead, and the marriage of Antipas with Herodias is not adultery in the strict sense of the word. It is again exceedingly difficult to imagine a Christian forger inventing so contradictory a statement.

(IV) At that time also a man came forward, if even it is fitting to call him a man. His nature as well as his form were a man's, but his showing forth was more than of a man. His works, that is to say, were godly, and he wrought wonder-deeds amazing and full of power. Therefore it is not possible for me to call him a man. But again, looking at the existence he shared with all, I would also not call him an angel.

And all that he wrought through some kind of invisible power, he wrought by word and command. Some said of him that our first Lawgiver has risen from the dead and shows forth many cures and arts. But others supposed that he is sent by God.

Now he opposed himself in much to the Law and did not observe the Sabbath according to ancestral custom. Yet on the other hand he did nothing reprehensible nor any crime, but by word solely he effected everything. And many from the folk followed him and received his teachings. And many souls became wavering, supposing that through him the Jewish tribes would set themselves free from the Roman hands.

Now it was his custom often to stop on the Mount of Olives facing the city. And there he avouched his cures to the people. And there gathered themselves to him of servants a hundred and fifty, but of the folk a multitude. But when they saw his power that he accomplished everything he would by word, they urged him that he should enter the city and cut down the Roman soldiers and Pilate, and rule over us. But that one scorned it.

And thereafter when knowledge of it came to the Jewish leaders, they gathered together with the High Priest and spake, We are powerless and weak to withstand the Romans. But as withal the bow is bent, we will go and tell Pilate what we have heard, and we will be without distress, lest if he hear it from others we be robbed of our substance and ourselves be put to the sword and our children ruined. And they went and told it to Pilate.

And he sent and had many of the people cut down. And he had that wonder-doer brought up. And when he had instituted a trial concerning him, he perceived that he is a doer of good but not an evil-doer, nor a revolutionary, nor one who aimed at power, and he set him free. He had, you should know, healed his dying wife. And he went to his accustomed place and wrought his accustomed works. And as again more folk gathered themselves together round him, then did he win glory through his works more than all.

The teachers of the Law were envenomed with envy and gave thirty talents to Pilate, in order that he should put him to death. And he after he had taken it, gave them consent that they should themselves carry out their purpose. And they took him and crucified him according to the ancestral law.

There are various points to notice here. The difficulty of the writer in assessing the personality of Jesus is striking; either a Christian or a Jewish antagonist would surely have been much more definite one way or the other. This puzzled and non-committal statement has to me a primitive and authentic tone about it. The stress on Christ's attitude to the Sabbath is significant and confirms the Gospel narrative. The number of 150 followers gathered on the Mount of Olives is interesting and quite credible, and the concern of the Jewish authorities at the way things seemed to be shaping is parallel to, but more definite than, John's account of a council meeting at this stage of the story (11, 47–53).

The real novelties here are – the statement that the Romans attacked and cut down some of the followers of Jesus, that he was then tried but released, and that subsequently Pilate was bribed to allow him to be crucified. It was on these points that Eisler laid such stress, as we saw in the last chapter, and while we cannot, of course, accept his extravagant theories, it may be that there was more political tension in Jerusalem at that time than we have often thought, and that this passage preserves an echo of it. The idea of Pilate being bribed is no doubt due to confusion with Judas's treachery. As to the closing sentence about the Jews taking Jesus and crucifying him, it is interesting to notice that the 'Apology of Aristides' (see p. 89) says, 'he was nailed on the cross by the Jews.'

(v) Again Claudius sent his authorities to those states – Cuspius Fadus and Tiberius Alexander, both of whom kept the people in peace, not allowing them to depart in anything from the pure laws. ... And at the time of these two, many had been discovered as servants of the previously described wonder-doer. And as they spake to the people about their teacher – that he is living, although he is dead, and that he will free you from your servitude – many from the folk gave ear to the above-named and took upon themselves their precept; not because of their reputation – they were indeed of the humbler sort, some just cobblers, others sandalmakers, others artisans. And yet as marvellous signs they accomplished in truth what they would.

But when those noble governors saw the misleading of the people, they deliberated with the scribes to seize and put them to death, for fear lest the little be not little if it have ended in the great. But they shrank back and were alarmed over the signs, saying, In the plain course such wonders do not occur. But if they do not issue from the counsel of God, they will be convicted quickly. And they gave them authority to act as they would. But afterwards becoming pestered by them, they had them sent away, some to the Emperor, but others to Antioch, others again to distant lands, for the testing of the matter.

This is a kind of précis of the story of the Early Church during the two decades following the crucifixion, and it is remarkable for the brief summary of the apostolic preaching – Christ risen and alive and able to liberate. The mention of the lowly trades followed by them and their converts is interesting, and the distinct reminiscence of Gamaliel's counsel (Acts 5, 38, 39) is strangely put in the mouth of the governors.

(VI) In the standard version of Josephus there is the familiar statement that inscriptions in Greek and Roman and Jewish characters were placed on pillars warning foreigners not to enter the inner court or holy place. In the Slavonic version there is this additional statement:

And over these tablets with inscriptions hung a fourth tablet with inscription in these characters to the effect – Jesus has not reigned as king; he has been crucified by the Jews, because he proclaimed the destruction of the city and the laying waste of the temple.

This is commonly thought to be an entirely imaginative statement without any basis in fact, but it does not appear to me to have very much value either as Christian or Jewish propaganda. Josephus's statement often used to be regarded with considerable scepticism, until in 1871 one of these inscriptions was discovered. Perhaps it is credulous to cherish a hope that a similar discovery may be made of one of these additional tablets!

(VII) This curtain was, prior to this generation, entire because the people were pious; but now it was lamentable to look at. It had, you should know, been suddenly rent from the top to the ground, when they delivered over to death through bribery the doer of good, the man – yea, him who through his doing was no man.

And of many other signs they tell which came to pass at that time. And it was said that after he was put to death, yea after burial in the grave he was not found. Some then assert that he is risen, but others that he has been stolen by his friends. I, however, do not know which speak more correctly.

For a dead man cannot rise of himself, though possibly with the help of another righteous man; unless it will be an angel or another of the heavenly authorities, or God himself appears as a man and accomplishes what he will, both walks with men and falls and lies down and rises up, as it is according to his will. But others said that it was not possible to steal him, because they had put guards all round his grave, thirty Romans but a thousand Jews.

Such is narrated as to that curtain. Moreover as to the cause of its tearing there are (? various statements).

The non-committal nature of these references to the resurrection would appear to exclude the possibility of this being a Christian interpolation. It feels much more like the comment of a puzzled Jew who knew one definite fact – the rending of the veil – and many rumours and much controversy regarding the resurrection. This of course leaves open the question whether it is primitive or medieval.

(VIII) In the ordinary texts of Josephus there is a prophecy of a world-ruler, and the name of Vespasian is associated with it, probably on the grounds that it was in Judea that he was made emperor. In the Slavonic version we read:

Some indeed by this understood Herod, but others the crucified wonder-doer Jesus, others again Vespasian.

It is an interesting fact that both Suetonius and Tacitus quote this ambiguous oracle, said to have been found in Jewish sacred writings, that 'about that time, one from their country should become governor of the habitable earth.'

Our brief examination of these passages has certainly not encouraged us to think that they are either Jewish or Christian additions for propagandist purposes. On the other hand, they have not convinced us that they really are primitive and therefore valuable fragments. But it does seem just possible that in some unexplained way they do preserve witness to the political tension in the lifetime of Jesus. And there at the moment we must leave the 'riddle of Josephus'.

CHAPTER 6

THE EVIDENCE OF THE TALMUD

———

JEWISH evidence regarding Jesus means not only the references in the works of Josephus, if they are indeed early and
authentic, but also those in the Talmud, such as they are.
We proceed now to examine these, following largely Dr
Joseph Klausner's admirable study *Jesus of Nazareth*.

The Talmud is a massive collection of Hebrew traditions,
interpretations of Scripture, comments and disputations,
illustrative tales and legends and folklore. In its present
completed form it dates from about A.D. 500, but it incorporates much earlier writing, and still earlier oral tradition.
The first and most important part of it is called the Mishna,
and it is a codification of the oral law which had gradually
grown up around the written Law of Moses during the last
century B.C. and the first two centuries A.D. This is in effect
'the tradition of the elders' of which we read (Mark 7, 3,
etc.); in the Gospel period it was in process of formation and
it was not finished until the beginning of the third century.
It is divided into sixty-three tractates or collections of material dealing with different themes, such as one regarding
the Sabbath. It is generally held to include first- and
second-century traditions of real value for the understanding
of the Judaism of the time of Jesus. The rabbinical authorities whose work is here preserved are known as the Tannaim.

In addition to the Mishna there is the Gemara, containing
large masses of material of all sorts collected by the Amoraim, or authorities from the third to the fifth centuries. It
is in two forms, one gathered at Jerusalem and the other in
Babylon, where there was a large Jewish population. The
Mishna plus the Jerusalem Gemara was completed in the
fourth century and is known as the Jerusalem Talmud; the
Mishna plus the Babylonian Gemara forms the Babylonian

Talmud and dates from a century later. While it is clearly to the Mishna that we turn for the earliest traditions, the position is somewhat complicated by the fact that some 'tannaitic' material is also found in the later strata of the Talmud and even outside it. However, for our purpose we obviously cannot enter into the intricacies of the matter but must follow the guidance of Klausner in examining what are apparently the earliest references to Jesus in the Talmud.

The first question that arises is under what name or names we are to look for him. It appears that he is mentioned many times explicitly by name – 'Yeshu of Nazareth', or by the term 'such-an-one' when a certain pseudonymity was desired because of Christian antagonism. He is also called 'Ben Pandera' from the scurrilous story current in the second century that his father was a Roman soldier of that name. Two other pseudonyms have commonly been thought to have been used, but Klausner rejects them both. There are passages where 'Balaam' apparently does not refer to the Old Testament character, and they have been supposed to be cryptic allusions to Jesus, but in several cases both names occur, which of course suggests that two different people are meant. The other term is 'Ben Stada', also explained as the name of a Roman soldier, but Klausner argues quite convincingly that such references are perhaps to the Egyptian prophet mentioned in Acts 21, 38, but certainly have nothing to do with Jesus.

Klausner examines the only twelve passages which he feels have any bearing on the question we are discussing – the contribution of the Talmud to our knowledge of Jesus. Of these he rules out four as of no value, leaving eight for us now to consider. His argument about the fewness of the references is of interest – the Talmud refers but rarely to the events of the period of the Second Temple, and only when such events were relevant to the legal and traditional matters in dispute. For example, there is no mention at all of Judas Maccabeus, and it is from the works of Josephus and from the two books of the Maccabees that we derive all our knowledge of the Maccabean revolt and struggle for freedom. It is not really remarkable then that there is no fuller study of the beginnings of Christianity.

(1) On the eve of Passover they hanged Yeshu of Nazareth, and the herald went before him for forty days saying, Yeshu of Nazareth is going forth to be stoned in that he hath practised sorcery and beguiled and led astray Israel. Let everyone knowing aught in his defence come and plead for him. But they found naught in his defence and hanged him on the eve of the Passover.

This of course agrees with the Gospel statement stating that the death of Jesus took place on the eve of the Passover (John 19, 14), and the word 'hanged' instead of 'crucified' is not a substantial difference, for the wider term is used several times in the New Testament (Acts 5, 30; 10, 39; 3, 13). The reference to sorcery clearly implies at least the miracles of healing and reminds us of the scornful jibe of the scribes: 'By the prince of the devils he casteth out devils' (Mark 3, 22, etc.). What we have here is a developed form of that attack. The distinctly new points are the reference to stoning – which is odd because it contradicts the earlier and subsequent reference to hanging – and the statements of the delay for forty days, the herald's challenge, and that no one came forward in answer to it and in support of Jesus. Klausner is quite clear that these latter statements are tendentious – that is to say, that they are unhistorical and deliberately framed to bolster up the Jewish view of the whole business. It must be remembered throughout that Klausner writes as a Jew not as a Christian.

(2) Jesus had five disciples, Mattai, Naqai, Netser, Buni, and Todah.

This is followed by a late addition from the times of the Amoraim, in which the meaning of these names is discussed in a semi-facetious manner, doubtless unhistorical and valueless. Mattai of course suggests Matthew; Naqai has been thought a corruption of Nicodemus; Todah is not unlike Thaddeus; Netser may be a confused reference to a Hebrew name for Christians generally; Buni is not far from Yuani, or John; but all this attempted identification seems unprofitable. The question of the number of the disciples being given as five, not twelve, is odd; Klausner appears to think it may be correct, the larger number being a Christian development in order to suggest the twelve tribes of Israel. This does not appear probable to me.

(3) An intending proselyte to Judaism called up the spirit of Jesus by spells to ask his advice. What is the most important thing in the world? he enquired, and the answer was – Israel. He then asked, And how if I should join myself with them? The reply was, Seek their good and do not seek their harm; everyone that hurteth them is as if he hurt the apple of God's eye.

A later note, however, speaks of Jesus as 'a transgressor in Israel', and 'a scoffer against the words of the wise'. While obviously unsatisfactory from a historical point of view, this passage and the next may have a certain value for the understanding of the attitude of the rabbis to Jesus.

(4) Rabbi Eliezer said, Balaam looked forth and saw that there was a man, born of a woman, who should rise up and seek to make himself God, and to cause the whole world to go astray. Therefore God gave power to the voice of Balaam that all the peoples of the world might hear, and thus he spake, Give heed that ye go not astray after that man; for it is written, God is not man that he should lie. And if he says that he is God he is a liar, and he will deceive and say that he departeth and cometh again at the end. He saith and he shall not perform.

This Rabbi Eliezer was one of the earliest and greatest of the Tannaim, having been born not long after the death of Jesus, so in this and other passages here in which he figures we may well be in touch with primitive ideas. While Jesus is not mentioned in this passage by name, the references to 'born of a woman' and 'making himself God' and 'departing and coming again' are sufficient indications that he is meant. It adds nothing to our knowledge of him, but does show aspects of the Gospel with which rabbis of the first centuries were familiar and against which they had to contend. The reference to causing the whole world to go astray is significant, as it implies the realization that Christianity was no merely personal or parochial affair but in the thought and purpose of Jesus was for all mankind.

(5) Rabbi Shimeon ben Azzai said, I found a genealogical roll in Jerusalem wherein was recorded, Such-an-one is a bastard of an adulteress.

This is apparently one of the oldest statements about Jesus in the Talmud, as this rabbi was a colleague of Rabbi Aqiba, who was killed in the Bar-Cochba rebellion (132). It of course represents the Jewish reply to Christian claims about the Virgin birth, and from the middle of the second century this was one of the chief points of argument between Jews and Christians. Klausner is quite emphatic that there is no historical foundation for the tradition of Jesus's illegitimate birth. It is uncertain whether birth records were kept in Jerusalem in those days, but even if there were the chances of their being fabricated or tampered with or misquoted are obviously enormous. We may notice the absence of any reference here to Pandera or any other supposed father – clearly that is a later development of this unpleasant lie.

(6) They asked Rabbi Eliezer, What of such-an-one as regards the world to come? He said to them, You have only asked me about such-an-one. What of a bastard as touching inheritance? What of him as touching the levirate duties? What of him as regards whitening his house? What of him as regards whitening his grave? Not because he evaded them by words, but because he never said a word which he had not heard from his teacher.

The point of interest here is that Eliezer evidently refused to make a pronouncement that Jesus had no part in the world to come; he had been taught nothing on the issue raised and therefore kept silent about it. As we have seen, Jesus was regarded as a transgressor of the Law, but this shows that he was not thought of as having forfeited all hope for the future. Similarly, the next two passages suggest that some orthodox Jews were still maintaining contact with the followers of Jesus at this time.

(7) When Rabbi Eliezer was an old man he was accused of leanings towards Christianity, but he explained the matter to

Rabbi Aqiba, one of his disciples, thus. Once I was walking along the upper market of Sepphoris and I found one of the disciples of Jesus of Nazareth, and Jacob of Kefar Sekanya was his name. He said to me, It is written in your law, Thou shalt not bring the hire of a harlot into the house of God (Deut. 23, 18). What was to be done with it – a latrine for the High Priest?. But I answered nothing. He said to me, Jesus of Nazareth taught me, For the hire of a harlot hath she gathered them and unto the hire of a harlot shall they return (Micah 1, 7); from the place of filth they come and unto the place of filth they shall go. And the saying pleased me and because of this I was arrested.

Klausner accepts this as an actual incident and an authentic saying of Jesus. He even thinks it possible that the Jacob mentioned was James, the Lord's brother and leader of the Church at Jerusalem (Acts 15, 13), whose martyrdom took place in 62. This must be deemed quite doubtful, but Eliezer may well have talked with some of those who knew Jesus during his lifetime, and this fact gives an added interest to this story.

The question discussed may perhaps seem unpleasant to us, but we must remember that there was a certain frankness of speech about bodily functions in those days and that Jesus himself spoke bluntly on occasion (Matt. 15, 17; Mark 7, 18, 19). And it should be noted that there is no attempt in the story to belittle Jesus – on the contrary his exposition of the point in question pleased the Rabbi.

(8) Imma Shalom, wife of Rabbi Eliezer, and her brother Gamaliel decided to make fun of a certain philosopher of Christian sympathies, who was said never to accept a bribe. She sent him a lamp of gold and asked him to pronounce in favour of her receiving a share of the family estate. He did so, and in reply to Gamaliel's objection that this was contrary to the Law he said, Since the day when you were driven from your country, the Law of Moses has been done away, and the Gospel has been given, in which it reads Son and daughter shall inherit together. The next day, Gamaliel brought to the philosopher a Libyan ass. He then said to them, I have looked further to the end of the book and it says, I am not come to take away from the Law of Moses, and I am not come to add to the Law of Moses. It stands written in the Law of Moses, Where there is a son, a daughter shall not inherit. Imma Shalom

said, Let your light shine as a lamp! But Rabbi Gamaliel said, The ass has come and has overturned the lamp!

Klausner thinks that there may be some substance in this amusing tale, and that the incident took place not long after the destruction of Jerusalem (70). If so, it is very early and valuable witness to the existence of Gospel material in writing in primitive times, and to the discussions and controversies which certainly occurred between the Christians and the Jews. The mingling of respect and ridicule here may be noted.

The Gospel references are interesting but perplexing. There is nothing in our Gospels corresponding to the words – 'Son and daughter shall inherit together.' It was not the practice normally of Jesus to legislate on matters of this kind (Luke 12, 14), but the words might be a deduction from something said by him on the equality of the sexes – which might also lie behind Paul's 'neither male nor female' (Gal. 3, 28). The second quotation seems like a garbled version of Matt. 5, 17, but of course that text does not come near the end of the Gospel as is stated here. It would be attractive to think that the book the philosopher had was one of the earlier source documents from which our Gospel was compiled, but it is of course more likely that it is just a case of slack quotation or sheer imagination. The fact, however, that there is also a reference to Matt. 5, 16 does seem to suggest that he was handling material covering that portion of the teaching of Jesus.

Klausner quotes one other story – which illustrates the practice of the second generation of disciples as to healing in the name of Jesus, to which there are also later references in the Talmud:

It happened to Rabbi Eliezer ben Dama that a serpent bit him, and Jacob of Kefar Sama came to heal him in the name of Yeshu ben Pandera. But Rabbi Ishmael, his uncle, forbade him, saying, Ben Dama, you are not permitted. He answered, I will bring thee proof that he may heal me. But ere he could bring a proof he died. Rabbi Ishmael said, Happy art thou, Ben Dama, that thou hast gone in peace, and has not broken down the fence of the wise.

Both Eliezer and Jacob were common Jewish names and probably those mentioned here were different from those in the previous anecdotes. By a 'proof' was no doubt meant a verse from the Law which could be interpreted as sanctioning the healing.

Apart from various small points of interest which have emerged in the course of this survey of the passages in the Talmud which refer to Jesus, there are two ways in which its evidence is of importance. (1) It shows clearly that the Rabbis of the first century who had every chance of knowing the truth, accepted the fact of the historicity of Jesus; they wrote against the Christian tradition in various respects, but they never denied its basis in actual historical events. (2) It helps us to see something of their attitude to Jesus and the first generation of Christians. Klausner maintains that, while there was criticism and scorn, there was not the same bitter hatred and hostility which we find later on. He says they were more averse to his followers than to Jesus himself, because in them they saw a danger to the national existence.

But a piece of evidence adduced by G. D. Kilpatrick in his book *Origins of the Gospel according to St Matthew* must be considered in this connexion. He quotes a Jewish prayer known as the Birkath ha-Minim, which he says was composed by Samuel the Small about 85, and says that in its earliest form it may be translated as follows:

> For the excommunicate let there be no hope and the arrogant government do thou swiftly uproot in our days; and may the Christians and the heretics suddenly be laid low and not be inscribed with the righteous. Blessed art thou, O Lord, who humblest the arrogant.

Kilpatrick calls Epiphanius and Jerome as witnesses that this prayer did include explicit mention of the Christians, and says that certain Genizah fragments from Cairo show this also. It is certainly a fairly blunt petition for the damnation of one's enemies, though not couched in the most violent of terms!

CHAPTER 7

EARLY ARCHAEOLOGICAL EVIDENCE

IT will of course be asked whether archaeology has anything to contribute to our investigation. During the last hundred years a great deal of exploration has taken place in Rome, Egypt, and elsewhere, and many important discoveries have been made of monuments, inscriptions, and documents which have thrown much light on many Biblical matters. The famous *Sayings of Jesus*, unearthed from rubbish heaps at Oxyrhynchus, will be studied in a later chapter. Meanwhile there are some still earlier fragments of possible information to be considered.

It is now known that the catacombs at Rome and some other cities were not, as was formerly thought, the hiding-places of the Christians where they could worship in secret. They may at times have been used in this way, but generally speaking they were the burial vaults and chambers in which the bodies of the dead were deposited. The explorations of de Rossi and others in the nineteenth century brought to light an enormous number of objects and relics of all kinds, and in particular sculptures, inscriptions, graffiti (words and drawings on walls), which give much information about the life and thought of the Christians at Rome during the first few centuries. Crude representations of scenes from the Gospels are found in great abundance, the Good Shepherd bearing the lost lamb being a first favourite.

It used to be stated rather confidently that some of this material was of first-century date. For example, the Rev. A. C. Jennings, in an appendix to Dr Foakes-Jackson's *History of the Christian Church* (1891), said, 'It is certain that these subterranean cemeteries take us back almost to the earliest days of Christianity at Rome. The catacomb of St Priscilla was probably the family burial-place of Pudens, a contemporary of the apostles. There is little doubt that the catacomb of Nereus and Achilleus was a bequest from the noble lady Domitilla, niece of the Emperor Vespasian, who was banished as a Christian by Trajan. ... The catacomb named later after Agnes (herself a martyr in the time of Diocletian) contains monuments assigned to the first century.' This I am afraid is an exaggeration. Later research may be represented by Jack Finegan's *Light from the Ancient Past* (1947), in the course of which he makes much use of Professor Paul Styger's investigations and accepts his conclusion that the oldest of the catacombs belong to a time around the middle of the second century.

It has long been held that Christianity penetrated in the first century into certain noble families at Rome. In addition to Domitilla, mentioned above, and her husband Clemens, who was beheaded for 'atheism' (a familiar charge levelled against Christians), there was Pomponia Graecina, wife of Aulus Plautius, commander of the Roman army in Britain, who was accused of 'foreign superstition' and retired into private life, and Acilius Glabrio, who was consul with Trajan in 91 and later died as a Christian. It is surely very significant that catacombs bearing these family names should date from less than a hundred years after the death of Paul. It is interesting that the name Priscilla was a customary one in the Acilian family, and we are reminded at once of Paul's friends, Aquila and Priscilla.

A point of particular interest is that in the catacomb of Priscilla one room, known as the Cappella Greca, or Greek Chapel, has the finest series of Christian wall paintings preserved in any single room in the catacombs (mid second century). In particular, there is a painting of the Resurrection of Lazarus in which Christ is shown – 'youthful and beardless, with short hair and large eyes. ... Although it is now only barely recognizable, this picture is of great interest since it is the oldest representation of Jesus that is preserved anywhere.'

While, then, the catacombs do not yield us much material for our study, though of very great interest in themselves and full of significance for the early history of the Church, they do certainly reinforce the general argument already advanced for the historicity of Jesus. If within little more than a hundred years after his death these extensive burial-places for Christians were being made and adorned with scenes from the Gospels and epitaphs and invocations, then there can be no substance in theories of myth and imagination regarding the origins of Christianity.

Reference may also be made to another portrayal of Christ, dating from early in the third century. It was found on the wall of a house-chapel at Dura-Europos in the Syrian Desert in 1931–2 during excavations by Yale University and the French Academy of Inscriptions and Letters, and is part of a representation of the Healing of the Paralytic. Jesus is shown standing over the bed, reaching out his hand to the man. Here too he is young and without a beard and wearing the ordinary costume of the time. Other pictures elsewhere in the third century show him still as youthful, but with long curly hair. It is not until the fourth century that the familiar bearded face appears.

There is one other piece of archaeological evidence to be considered – the famous *Sator* formula discovered at Pompeii and elsewhere. This odd collection of words was for long used as a magic charm which was believed to have value against the bites of snakes and dogs, and in promoting easy childbirth. Its strange real significance seems only recently to have been unravelled, if indeed it has been – for by no means all scholars are convinced that the suggested solution is correct.

The usual form of it, found widely from the fifth century onwards throughout the Middle Ages, is as follows:

```
S A T O R
A R E P O
T E N E T
O P E R A
R O T A S
```

It is of course a complete word square, but it is more than

that – it is also a perfect palindrome, i.e. a sentence reading in exactly the same way from left to right and from right to left, thus:

SATOR AREPO TENET OPERA ROTAS

Before we deal with the question of its meaning, it must be noticed that there is another form of it in which the order of the words is reversed:

R O T A S
O P E R A
T E N E T
A R E P O
S A T O R

The few examples of this that have been found are earlier in date than the others and it is probable for a reason which will be mentioned later that this is the original form of the square.

An immense literature has gathered about this formula, chiefly on the continent. The best English studies of it are two articles by Professor Donald Atkinson, of the University of Manchester, to whom I am indebted for the information given here. The first appeared in the *Bulletin of the John Rylands Library*, October 1938, and the second in the *Journal of Ecclesiastical History*, January 1951.

In the ROTAS form it was discovered in 1868 cut into a fragment of wall-plaster from a Roman ruin at Cirencester, in Gloucestershire, and it is deemed to date from the fourth century during the Roman occupation of Britain. It may be seen in the Cirencester museum. In 1925 an incomplete example of it was found during excavations at Pompeii, and as the destruction of Pompeii by the eruption of Vesuvius took place in A.D. 79, the origin of the square would seem to antedate that event and be much earlier than had been supposed. Another and complete example was discovered also at Pompeii in 1936, scratched on the plaster of a column of the palaestra, or campus. About the same time four examples of it were found during the excavations at Dura-Europos conducted by Yale University and the French

Academy; they are confidently dated to the first half of the
third century and regarded as the work of soldiers belonging
to the Roman garrison stationed there, as is known, at that
time.

Now as to the meaning of this cryptic sentence. It is, unfortunately, not entirely clear, because the word 'arepo' is
unknown in Latin, but it is generally thought to represent a
Celtic word for plough. In which case the sentence says
something about the sower or farmer holding with labour
the wheels of the plough, which might well be a mysterious
reminder of the Creator controlling the rotation of the sea-
sons and holding all things in the hollow of his hand. But
that seems of little interest or importance to us. If that were
all that could be unravelled from these odd words it would
not be worth our attention here. It is because there is almost
certainly another meaning hidden in it of very considerable
significance that we are including it in our study.

In 1926 a German scholar, Grosser, made an astonishing
discovery – that from these twenty-five letters the first two
words of the Lord's Prayer in Latin can be made twice, but
in such a way that the letter N, which appears only once,
stands as the middle letter of a cross. Thus:

```
                    P
                    A
                    T
                    E
                    R
        P A T E R N O S T E R
                    O
                    S
                    T
                    E
                    R
```

This leaves four letters, A twice and O twice; we shall refer to
these presently, after endeavouring to explain how this
strange phenomenon can have come about. Mathematicians
say that the chances against an accidental occurrence of this

sort are too high to be seriously considered – there must be purpose behind it.

It would appear then that the square was deliberately framed out of these twenty-five letters to enshrine in a secret and mysterious way words and ideas that belong to the very heart of the Christian faith. We may surmise that the original author in the first place arranged the two sacred words PATER NOSTER in the form of a cross, perhaps writing them on an actual cross of wood or even of papyrus, as a kind of holy remembrancer or aid to devotion. Then in a time of persecution – perhaps the Neronian – he framed the square to contain yet conceal the beloved teaching. Lacking four letters, however, for a five-word square, he very skilfully chose the other two sacred letters, A and O, reminding of the lovely words 'I am Alpha and Omega' (Rev. 1, 11), and repeated them twice. The very fact which we have noticed of the difficulty about the word 'arepo' and of getting an exact and satisfactory interpretation of the sentence may itself point in this direction – he did his best within the limits of the available letters, but the result was not entirely perfect.

Two other points may be mentioned. It has been suggested that if the squares are marked out in this simple unobtrusive way there would be given a veiled hint of their Christian significance:

R O	T	A S			S A	T	O R
O P	E	R A			A R	E	P O
T E	N	E T			T E	N	E T
A R	E	P O			O P	E	R A
S A	T	O R			R O	T	A S

If, as we have suggested, the first of these forms is the older and more original, it may well have been felt that the o's and a's are badly placed and that the reversed order with the a's in the top left of the square and the o's beneath or at the right is more satisfactory – which would explain why this form presently became the more popular. We should notice too the hint of the Cross through the arrangement of the two TENET's is reinforced by the very fact that the letter T is equivalent to the Greek letter Tau, which at any rate from early in the second century was used as a symbol of the Cross. To the instructed, then, we may say, the square was full of Christian meaning and suggestion.

Now all this is not just a matter of curious interest – it is of first-rate importance for our study, and indeed for the whole question of Christian origins. For if the Rotas-Sator square is indeed a concealed form of the opening words of the Lord's Prayer in Latin then these two Pompeian graffiti may be the earliest extant pieces of Christian writing. Presumably written before 79, they ante-date by several decades the oldest papyrus scraps of Gospel material, which as we shall see in a later chapter probably date from early in the second century. That the Prayer was known and used in Latin at such an early date is remarkable, but even more so is the fact that the Greek letters Alpha, Omega, and Tau were apparently, with their Latin equivalents, already symbols of Christ.

Naturally this reading of the square and its significance has been much disputed. Other interpretations have been suggested – that it is Jewish (with some link with the wheels of Ezekiel 1), or Mithraic, or Orphic. But none of these have found much acceptance, and Atkinson argues convincingly against them. They all put a great strain on our belief in coincidence. Another line of attack has been that, some time later than 79, clandestine searchers for treasure amongst the ruins may have scratched these squares on the walls, but Atkinson equally disposes of this suggestion. Finally, it has been argued that the presence of Christians at Pompeii at such an early date is extremely improbable.

That may be true, but it is by no means certain. Many improbable things prove to be facts! As long ago as 1824 a drawing of a cross was found on a wall at Pompeii, and in 1864 de Rossi published an inscription which apparently referred to Christians. More recently an imprint of a cross has been discovered, in a house at Herculaneum, not far distant from Pompeii and destroyed by the same eruption of

Vesuvius. And as Atkinson says, 'If a cross and so a Christian at Herculaneum, why not a cross and other Christians at Pompeii?' After all, Paul found 'brethren' at Puteoli, not very far away (Acts 28, 14).

I do not propose to study here the question of sacred sites in Palestine and elsewhere. Some identifications may be regarded as reasonably certain, though a measure of doubt often remains. For example, Tell Hum, on the north-west side of the Sea of Galilee, is commonly considered the site of ancient Capernaum, but the ruins of the synagogue there probably date from the second century; they may stand on the site of an earlier building, that mentioned in the Gospels, but they are not themselves the remains of it. But even if identification may be deemed fairly definite, this is not proof that the recorded incidents actually happened there. The most it can do is to encourage belief in the historicity of the narrative and perhaps elucidate certain aspects of it. The fact that Jacob's Well was probably where tradition asserts is no proof that Jesus sat there, though it may add some local colour to the story. The same applies to other sites, such as Gethsemane and Golgotha.

One comparatively recent 'find' must be mentioned, though its exact significance is still in doubt. In September 1945, Professor Sukenik of the Hebrew University at Jerusalem – whose name is familiar through the discovery of the Dead Sea Scrolls – was responsible for excavations at Talpioth, a suburb of Jerusalem, and in a burial chamber there he found two ossuaries, or receptacles for bones, on which he read the name 'Jesus'. It is confidently stated that 'these graffiti must have been executed before the middle of the first Christian century.' They were at first thought to be laments over the death of Jesus, but an alternative explanation is that they are prayers addressed to him on behalf of some person buried there, 'Jesus, let him arise.' Whichever view is correct, it certainly is most remarkable to find such very early testimony to him, and it encourages the hope that more and better evidence will yet be found from the first decades after the crucifixion. My authority for this note is an article by Dr B. Gustafsson of Lund in the November (1956) issue of *New Testament Studies*.

We may sum up this study by saying that early archaeological evidence of the beginnings of Christianity is not lacking, though it is not yet as extensive or conclusive for the earliest period as we could wish. Considered alone it may not be very impressive, but as one link in a chain consisting of much literary and historical witness it undoubtedly has a place. And we cherish the expectation that still more valuable discoveries will presently be made.

CHAPTER 8

THE UNCANONICAL SAYINGS

———

THE pagan and Jewish evidence we have been considering has been almost entirely of a confirmatory nature, very little additional information about Jesus coming to us from these sources. Coming now to Christian writers later than the New Testament, the position is reversed – there is so much support for the facts of the Gospel that it is impossible to deal with it. It is for 'extras' that we now search, and in particular for agrapha and uncanonical stories told about Jesus.

Before proceeding to examine various groups of these there are two general points to be considered. The first is as to the credibility of authentic material of this kind surviving at all, and the second as to how its genuineness may be tested. We deal with the first of these questions in this chapter, and the second in the next.

As already mentioned, the word 'agrapha' means literally 'unwritten things'. It was used originally in Greek by some ancient writers as a description of traditions which were orally transmitted, but this is no longer implied by its use, for obviously all this material has been found written somewhere. Its significance nowadays is therefore that it was not included in the official writings recognized by the Church as Gospels. We may call the agrapha 'uncanonical sayings' if we like, as I have done in the chapter heading here, so long as we remember that it is the Gospel canon to which we refer, for as we saw in Chapter 2 there are a number of such passages in the New Testament elsewhere than in the Gospels. Sometimes the term 'apocryphal sentences' has been used, but, as we shall see later, there are objections to this. It seems much better to have a technical expression like 'agrapha' which exactly describes them.

It was Alfred Resch, the German scholar, who brought

the word into current use with the publication of his comprehensive and erudite study of this material in 1889; his own theory of the origin of these sayings – that they came from a primitive document not now extant which was also the groundwork of the Synoptic Gospels – has not been generally accepted, but his book has been the quarry in which all later writers have worked. Probably the best study of the subject in English has been the article entitled 'Agrapha' in Hastings's *Dictionary of the Bible* (extra volume) by J. H. Ropes, but many smaller collections of them have been made. Many years ago Farrar included a brief list in an appendix to his *Life of Christ*, as did Stubbs in his *Verba Christi*. Dr M. R. James, in *The Apocryphal New Testament*, has sections dealing with the agrapha, the papyrus sayings, and the fragments of the Hebrew Gospel, which are all closely allied. My own book, *The Unwritten Gospel*, contains a considerable collection of such passages.

The most varied opinions have been held as to the genuineness of this material. In his first study Resch enumerated seventy-five sayings which he regarded as probably genuine, but he modified this somewhat in a later edition. Ropes considered him much too sanguine; of the sixty-six sayings he studies he thinks only ten have historical value, and that a good but not conclusive case can be made out for twenty-four others. Such a measure of hesitation and scepticism may be taken as fairly typical. On the other hand, Dr Rendel Harris, a great worker in this field of study, considered that some of these passages are so valuable that (as I mentioned in our first chapter) they should be gathered into an appendix to the New Testament. And Dr David Smith, a scholar-preacher, in a little book entitled *Unwritten Sayings of our Lord* (1913), spoke of an appreciation of these sayings being 'a pious duty to our Lord', some of them being so well attested that it is 'impiety to slight them'.

A strong case against the likelihood of there being many genuine agrapha has, however, been argued on the following grounds. The conditions under which the Church grew up militated against the careful retention and faithful transmission of the details of what Jesus said and did. There was a strong expectation that the end of the age was imminent and that the appearance of Christ in glory would take place within that very generation. Why then should records have been made of what had happened in the past? Their eyes were upon the heavenly future and they had no anticipation of future generations on earth requiring information about the life and sayings of Jesus. When this apocalyptic expectation proved mistaken and narratives began to be made (the earliest of the Gospels, St Mark, is usually dated between 60 and 70) the gap between the Aramaic-speaking first Christians of Palestine and the Greek-speaking converts in Greece and Rome was so great that historical reminiscence from the earliest days would probably be slight. And the likelihood is that what there was of it was gathered into the canonical Gospels, with very little if anything left over.

But against this there are a number of considerations that compel attention.

(1) In the first place, there was a period before this expectation arose when Jesus was regarded as a great prophet (Luke 7, 16, etc.), and it would be the most natural thing in the world for his followers to begin to preserve in writing records of the things he was saying and doing, just as Baruch had done in the case of Jeremiah. St Luke is thought to have kept a travel diary of his journeyings with St Paul, and I can see no reason why the same may not have been true of one or more of the first disciples.

(2) For it must be remembered that writing was not a rare and specialized achievement in the first century – it was freely and familiarly employed, as the vast discoveries of papyri have proved. Even systems of shorthand in Greek and Latin were used, and Dr A. T. Robertson goes so far as to say, 'Business man as Matthew was, he could easily have taken down in Aramaic shorthand notes of discourses of Jesus.' The remark that the apostles were 'unlearned and ignorant men' (Acts 4, 13) does not contradict this idea, but probably just means that they were uninstructed in the subtleties of the Rabbinical schools.

(3) Moreover, many purely personal motives might operate to produce and preserve such documents, men handing on to their descendants accounts of what had happened. 'Would not the grandsons of the man born blind or of him who had been healed of a withered hand tell about this?' it has been asked. And the more widely belief in Jesus spread and the more highly honoured he became, the greater would be the joy individuals would find in recollecting and retelling incidents in which they had shared. We may recall Paul's statement that above five hundred brethren had witnessed an appearance of the risen Lord 'of whom the greater part remain unto this present' (1 Cor. 15, 6).

(4) Further, even after the apocalyptic hope had come to dominate the Church's thought and teaching, interest in the earthly life of Jesus would certainly have been maintained and records of it preserved either in writing or by oral transmission. For the preaching of the apostles and their successors was not simply that *a* man had been raised from the dead, but that *this* man 'approved of God among you by miracles and wonders and signs', and wickedly murdered, had conquered death and was still offering remission of sins and the gift of life. And in this preaching some explanation must also have been given of what repentance meant – the new way of life and the higher code of morals to which Christ called them.

For all these reasons, then, I cannot take the view that there is any improbability about the idea that sayings of Jesus may have continued to circulate either in writing or in speech for many decades after his death, and so presently have found their way into uncanonical books from which now we may extract them. Dealing with one particular group of agrapha which we shall consider in due course, those found in old manuscripts of the Gospels, Canon Streeter says, 'The antecedent probability that some traditions as to the sayings and deeds of Christ, not included in any of the Gospels, would have been in circulation in the early Church, is high, and it would be very natural to record them in the margin of a Gospel, from whence they might

easily slip into the text.' A more general statement of Dr
J. H. Moulton may be added, 'When we think of those three
years which were so crowded with teaching, whereof a mere
fraction is preserved for us in the Gospels, and think moreover how many thousands heard the great Teacher speak
and passed on to their children and grandchildren the well-
remembered sayings which fastened on their memory, our
wonder must surely be that so few traditional words of Jesus
have come down to us.'

To this general argument some other considerations may
be added which suggest a larger mass of available material
in the background. There is no proof of course that it was all
authentic, but there is surely a presumption that some of it
was. There are first of all traces within the Gospels themselves. The implication of the preface to St Luke's Gospel
(1, 1–4) is that some considerable literary activity had already taken place when he wrote, based on the reminiscences
of those who had seen and heard Jesus. And there is the
reference to 'many other things which Jesus did' in the
closing words of the Fourth Gospel (John 21, 25), which, it
has been well said, 'suggests the consciousness of the end of
the first century that the known material was not exhausted
in known writings.'

Indirect evidence of this larger body of evangelic matter
is found when we analyse the Gospels. It is usually now
held as a result of modern Biblical study that the writers of
Matthew and Luke both made use of a document not now
extant (commonly called 'Q' for convenience' sake), and
that each of them drew also from a source peculiar to himself. This means that there were three collections of stories
and sayings at that time which have not survived as entities
but the bulk of which are incorporated in our Gospels. The
obvious probability is that there was in each case a residue
of matter which they did not use; surely some of this may
have come down to us through other channels.

Again, the marginal notes in the Revised Version reveal
the fact that certain passages were no part of the Gospels at
first, but that they were added from some outside source or

sources – we may call them the 'waifs and strays' of the Gospel tradition. The two most important are the last twelve verses of Mark, and the story of the adulterous woman (John 7, 53–8, 11). The evidence is altogether against either of these belonging originally where it is now found, but not against them being added from some good extraneous source. It is quite credible then that, while some such material may now be irrecoverable, some other similar passages, though unsuccessful in attaching themselves to the canon, may nevertheless have survived as agrapha, embedded in other ancient writings.

Finally, there are certain statements by early writers which definitely picture the process of oral transmission at work over and beyond the written Gospels. The most important is the famous passage quoted by Eusebius in which Papias (who wrote about 130) described how he compiled his *Expositions of the Sayings of the Lord*. This work is not now extant – a few extracts only from it remain – but it is one of the lost documents, like the Hebrew Gospel, which may turn up any day as part of some archaeological discovery in Egypt or elsewhere. 'But I shall not be unwilling,' he said, 'to put down, along with my interpretations, whatsoever instructions I received with care in my memory, assuring you at the same time of their truth. ... If then anyone who had attended on the elders came, I asked minutely after their sayings, what Andrew or Peter said, or what was said by Philip or by Thomas or by James or by John or by Matthew or any other of the Lord's disciples, which things Aristion and the presbyter John, the disciples of the Lord, say. For I imagined that what was to be got from books was not so profitable to me as what came from the living and abiding voice.' Eusebius makes the following comment upon this passage: 'Papias gives also other accounts of the words of the Lord on the authority of Aristion who was mentioned above, and traditions as handed down by the presbyter John, to which we refer those who are fond of learning. ... The same writer gives also other accounts which he says came to him through unwritten tradition, certain strange parables and teachings of the Saviour, and some other more mythical things.' There are some puzzling features about this statement into which we cannot enter, but it is of great interest because it mentions two personal disciples of Jesus outside the apostolic company and says they contributed their quota to the repository of reminiscences which Papias compiled.

A briefer statement may be added from Clement of Alexandria (about 200); referring to those whom he was privileged to meet and hear, he says, 'They, preserving the tradition of the blessed doctrine derived directly from the holy apostles, Peter, James, John, and Paul, the son receiving it from the father, came by God's will to us also to deposit those ancestral and apostolic seeds.'

Many agrapha will be found in the following chapters, but meanwhile a few not subsequently dealt with may be quoted here:

I am the gate of life; he who entereth through me, entereth into life.

Keep the flesh pure and the seal unspotted that ye may receive life.

Woe to them that have not shewn mercy, for there they shall not receive mercy.

Thou hast seen thy brother, thou hast seen thy Lord.

Buy for yourselves, O ye children of Adam, through these transitory things which are not yours, that which is yours which does not pass away.

To sum up then: Jesus must of course have said and done far more than has been recorded in the Gospels. While circumstances militated against very much of this being preserved, the likelihood is that some of it would find its way into documents of different kinds. When therefore we find such material scattered through the literature of the first few centuries we naturally treat it with respect – and cherish the hope that some of it may be authentic. To the question of the genuineness or otherwise of these evangelic fragments we must now address ourselves.

CHAPTER 9

TESTS OF GENUINENESS

———

WE have argued that there is a real likelihood of some genuine agrapha having been in existence in the first few centuries after Christ, and that some of them may be found in early Christian literature. This does not of course mean that we can easily accept any saying ascribed to Jesus or story told of him as true. There are many ways in which the ascription may be a mistake, and it is important that we should glance at this point before proceeding to the difficult question of testing this material.

Sometimes unintentional errors have caused sayings to be wrongly included in lists of agrapha. A sentence in the Epistle of Barnabas used to be quoted thus: 'Let us resist all iniquity and hold it in hatred, as saith the son of God', but presently it was discovered that the true reading was 'as befits sons of God'. Sometimes sayings may have been elaborated unconsciously as they have passed from one to another – we all know how such exaggerations and embellishments of true incidents take place. There is also what Moffatt calls 'the plus of preaching', when happy thoughts intended to bring stories vividly before hearers catch on and become accepted as authentic. Another unintentional error is due to inaccurate quotation from books, which of course was much more likely to happen in olden times, when it was less easy to turn up and verify passages. Or again, texts may be accurately quoted but wrongly ascribed, as when words of Paul are attributed to Jesus.

But intentional inaccuracies have also to be reckoned with. It was the regular practice of Greek historians to compose speeches for their heroes if they had no record of what they had said on occasions which seemed to require some utterance – such as a general's exhortation before battle.

And so religious fiction came to be manufactured, often with the best of motives; Tertullian tells of a presbyter in Asia who confessed to the writing of the *Acts of Paul* from love of the apostle. And from that it is evidently an easy step to heretical manipulations of Gospel passages and the wholesale manufacture of apocryphal books. The growth of legend is a most interesting phenomenon and one that must certainly be reckoned with in such a study as this. Nevertheless, such considerations should not be so emphasized as to make us neglect the cogent arguments of the opposite character already advanced.

Clearly some kind of tests for genuineness must be devised and applied, though it may be stated at once that nothing of a conclusive nature is possible. The very fact that such scholars as Resch and Ropes have differed so greatly is an indication of that. The subjective factor is bound to enter into the matter at various stages. Everyone must assess the evidence as best he can, but personal bias cannot be entirely eliminated. It is not a question of mathematical or logical proof but of balancing probabilities, and about that opinions are certain to differ.

The most careful attempt to formulate principles of criticism in this matter is that of Ropes; the process that he outlines may be summarized thus, though he does not enumerate the points in exactly this way:

(1) The determination whether or not a passage is actually an agraphon, and not so described in error.

(2) The genealogical grouping of the authorities for a saying, to find the earliest known source (or sources, if two or more are independent).

(3) The enquiry whether this author (or these authors) may reasonably be thought to have had access to trustworthy tradition.

(4) The testing of the saying by what we know from the Gospels of the thought and spirit of Jesus.

(5) If as a result of this investigation the saying be rejected as not genuine, the search for a fair explanation of its evolution.

It is not necessary to try to improve on this, but some brief comment may be made on each of his points.

(1) We have already dealt above with the various ways in which errors, both unintentional and deliberate, may have caused sayings to be regarded as agrapha. Many other examples might be given – one will suffice. In the earliest known list of agrapha, that of a Belgian monk, Hubert Phalesius, in 1642, there is included the statement that the publican in the Gospel said, 'Lord, I a sinner am not worthy to lift my eyes to heaven.' It will readily be agreed that this is merely a misquotation of Luke 18, 13, and of no value. It is possible of course that variations in the way sayings are quoted may be due to different lines of tradition in some way – there is evidence of this in the Gospels. But there are a great many others, of which the above is one, which seem definitely to be just mistakes.

(2) On the second point Ropes says, 'The agrapha were much copied by ancient writers from one another, and even an imposing array of attesting authorities is in most cases reducible to one.' There may be some exaggeration here, for there is often much doubt as to whether one writer is dependent upon another or not. For example, part of the passage in the Epistle of Clement on commensurate judgements (which we shall notice in the next chapter) is also found in Polycarp and in Clement of Alexandria; did they borrow it from him? Dr Rendel Harris thought not, and argued that we thus had three early witnesses for it, but other scholars have disagreed. This point is therefore one that must be borne in mind, and we must not too readily assume that the evidence for a saying or the suggestion that it is genuine are increased because more than one example of it has been found. But the question is an intricate one and we need not consider it further.

(3) The third of Ropes's points requires fuller consideration because it seems to rule out too much too easily. He appears to dispose of the possibility of 'access to trustworthy tradition' in altogether too cavalier a fashion. He says that Papias (130–140) or Justin (150) – both of whom

we shall consider in the next chapter – may be allowed to have been in touch with reliable information, but not a fourth-century writer. But such a distinction is quite untenable, for there are numerous ways in which such a writer or later writers still may have had early and authentic material – no longer extant – on which to draw.

The question obviously has to be asked – how long did Papias's *Expositions* continue to circulate? There is no conceivable reason why a fourth-century writer may not have taken agrapha from him without acknowledging his source, so that though we have no clue to the fact we may in reading such a book or even something written later still be catching whispers from the earliest days. Now, a seventh- or eighth-century epitome, based probably on the *Chronicle of Philip of Side* (430), affirms that Papias in his second book told how John and James were both slain by the Jews, and a similar statement is also found in the best manuscript of the *Chronicle of Georgios Hamartolos* in the ninth century.

But Papias's book may have been extant later even than that. A volume is known to have been in the Church of Nîmes about 1218, which is described thus: 'The Book of Papias, The Book of the Words of the Lord.' Again, there may have been a copy in England also in the fifteenth century, for John Boston, a monk and bibliographer of Bury, includes 'Papias of Hierapolis' in the list of writers whose works he had seen in monastic libraries. There is also some other evidence suggesting the continued use of Papias down to Reformation times.

There are other facts of the same kind. The *Gospel according to the Hebrews* almost certainly contained some genuine agrapha which we will study in a later chapter, and as we shall see there it probably remained extant till the thirteenth century. Again, the apocryphal *Gospel of Peter*, written about 150, though heretical and not fully trustworthy, apparently incorporated traditions also used by Justin. A fragment of it survives in an eighth-century manuscript, and Dr James thinks another dates from the thirteenth. Yet again, certain Gospel manuscripts written in the twelfth century are thought to preserve readings current in Caesarea when Origen went there in 231.

All this means that Ropes's acceptance of Papias and Justin as possibly good witnesses to sound extra-canonical tradition carries with it as a corollary the possibility that very much later writers may have borrowed from them. It may be quite impossible to trace the links in the chain, but we cannot rule out later agrapha merely on that ground. A sceptical attitude regarding them is quite understandable, but 'not proven' is really a better verdict, remembering that later evidence may be unearthed some day.

(4) We come now to the fourth point – the question of the spiritual agreement or otherwise of agrapha with the known teaching of Jesus. Ropes's statement may be accepted regarding the importance of this aspect of our enquiry. It is, he says, on the answer to the question 'whether the saying is conceivable in the mouth of Jesus' that the ultimate decision depends. But at the same time the value of this test is strictly limited – it is more useful on the negative side than on the positive. It is certainly of use in ruling out some passages as unauthentic; comparatively early material may be felt to be so incongruous on the lips of Jesus that we feel we have no option but to reject it. But of course the subjective factor enters here again – there are bound to be great diversities of view about this. And still less on the positive side can we speak with complete confidence. We cannot make harmony with the known mind of Christ a substitute for weakness of attestation; the utmost we can say is that there is nothing in the sense or spirit of a saying that forbids us to think that Jesus may have said it, but that till more evidence comes to light it must remain an interesting 'perhaps'. It is as necessary to exercise care here as on the previous point, where absence of early evidence for a saying was shown not to be conclusive against its authenticity, in view of the many possibilities of late writings really reproducing quite early matter. Which means of course that this part of our study must of necessity deal with possibilities and probabilities rather than with certainties.

(5) The last point appears, as Ropes frames it, to have an academic rather than a practical value; our study of a saying may strictly be incomplete without an understanding of its origin and how it came to be ascribed to Jesus, but if our purpose is to sift the genuine from the false, our interest largely goes when we are convinced that a saying is spurious. And in any case very few of us have either the time or the inclination to probe so deeply into the matter. But at the same time possible explanations do sometimes occur to us of the sources of sayings and the reasons why they have been attributed to Jesus. Due weight must be given to such suggestions, though care must be taken not easily to prejudge the issue.

One example of this may be given. Origen makes this interesting statement:

Jesus therefore said, For the sake of the weak was I weak, for the sake of the hungry was I hungry, for the sake of the thirsty was I thirsty.

Now the brilliant suggestion has been made that no agraphon was intended at all – that is, that Origen was not claiming to quote an uncanonical word of Jesus. The idea is that we should punctuate it like this:

Jesus, therefore, said for the sake of the weak, I was weak, for the sake of the hungry, I was hungry, for the sake of the thirsty, I was thirsty.

In other words it is just a reference to Matthew 25, 35, 36, explaining that in that parable Jesus spoke as he did to encourage different groups of people. But attractive as this sounds it is by no means necessarily correct. There is no reference in the Gospel to the weak, the tenses of the verb are different, the order of the clauses is not the same – and more particularly, it was not for the sake of the distressed people that the parable was spoken but for those who aided them. Moreover, Paul's reference to the weakness of Christ (2 Cor. 13, 4) and to his own becoming weak (1 Cor. 9, 22) would be very apt if such a saying as this was known to him

– and this seems at least as reasonable a hypothesis as the other. Personally I consider it to be a genuine saying of Jesus.

Finally, it may be asked whether any help is to be found on this question of genuineness from an attempt to find a consensus of opinion. The answer is, I suggest, in the negative. As already mentioned, a considerable number of lists of agrapha have been drawn up – over fifty are known to me personally. But while there is a measure of agreement about some few sayings, one constantly feels regarding many of those for which there is no consensus, that this point or that has not been sufficiently considered by those who reject them. At the moment, then, we must rely upon our own judgement and make our own decisions even more in this matter than in most other realms of study.

CHAPTER 10

EARLY CHURCH WRITERS

—

THERE are several groups of books from which agrapha have been gleaned and we proceed now to examine these in turn. First of all we have the early Church writers commonly called the Apostolic Fathers; then the apologies and dialogues of those whom I have called in the next chapter 'Defenders of the Faith'; then next the apocryphal and secondary Gospels; then a collection of miscellaneous passages from later books; then agrapha from Gospel manuscripts; and finally those from fragments of papyrus discovered in modern times by archaeologists.

By the Apostolic Fathers are meant writers or writings (the term is used in both ways) of approximately the first hundred years after the Crucifixion. There is no fixed and agreed list of these, but the general significance of the expression is understood. Several of them have been found in certain ancient manuscripts of the New Testament, dating from a time when the canon was not yet definitely settled; that shows the high regard in which they were held.

(1) *The First Epistle of Clement* is probably the earliest of these documents. It was written from the Church at Rome to the Church at Corinth about the year 95; the name of Clement is not actually mentioned, but the ascription is ancient and generally accepted. Eusebius, the historian of the early Church, speaks of Clement as the third bishop of Rome, and identifies him with the Clement mentioned by Paul (Phil. 4, 3), but this is regarded as very doubtful. The epistle reproves the lack of humility amongst the Corinthians and stresses the humble-mindedness of Jesus. For our purpose only two passages need be cited:

Most of all remembering the words of the Lord Jesus which he spake, teaching forbearance and longsuffering; for thus he spake,

Have mercy that ye may receive mercy; forgive that it may be forgiven you; as ye do, so shall it be done to you; as ye give, so shall it be given to you; as ye judge, so shall ye be judged; as ye show kindness, so shall kindness be shown unto you; with what measure ye mete, it shall be measured withal to you.

Remember the words of our Lord Jesus, for he said, Alas for that man! It would have been better for him if he had never been born than to make one of my chosen fall. He might better have had a millstone hung around his neck and have been sunk in the sea than to pervert one of my chosen.

It is impossible to be sure whether these are loose quotations from the Gospels or – especially in the first case – alternative accounts of the teaching of Jesus, perhaps on some different occasion. In any case it is very early evidence regarding this important emphasis of his.

(2) The *Didache* (pronounced 'did-ah-key'), or 'Teaching of the Twelve Apostles', was discovered in a Greek manuscript in 1873, and was soon felt to be a very ancient and valuable document – not actually the work of the apostles themselves but certainly representing primitive tradition regarding what they thought and taught. A shorter, simpler form of the same teaching has long been known in Latin, and it has usually been supposed that this was a sort of précis of the *Didache*. It has recently been argued by the American scholar, Dr Edgar Goodspeed, in his book *The Apostolic Fathers*, that this Latin version is really the more original – though no doubt a translation of a Greek composition. He calls it 'The Doctrina' to distinguish it from the later and fuller *Didache*. He thinks it was written about the year 100, in which case it is, after the Epistle of Clement, the next oldest Christian document outside the New Testament. But most scholars do not accept his theory.

It comprises a series of short commands regarding the Two Ways – the Way of Life and the Way of Death. The opening paragraph says,

The Way of Life is this: first, you shall love the eternal God who made you; second, your neighbour as yourself. Moreover, anything that you would not have done to you, you shall not do to anyone else.

This is of course a variant form of Christ's teaching about the two great commandments, and a negative form of the Golden Rule (Matt. 22, 37–9; 7, 12). Some of the precepts and prohibitions that follow are familiar to us – from the Ten Commandments and the Sermon on the Mount, but some strike a new note. A few may be quoted:

Do not be a grumbler, for it leads to cursing.

Do not keep stretching out your hands to receive, and drawing them back when it comes to returning.

Do not be an astrologer or an enchanter, which things lead to idolatry, and do not want to look at them or hear them.

Reconcile those who are quarrelling.

You shall hate all hypocrisy, and you shall not do anything that is not pleasing to the Lord.

If you do these things daily with reflection, you will be near the Living God, but if you do not do them, you will be far from the truth.

These are not stated to be the words of Jesus – indeed his name only occurs once, in the closing sentence of the book, but their kinship to his teaching is obvious and they seem fairly natural elaborations of it. Dr Goodspeed is of the opinion that they are a sort of Jewish-Christian counterblast to the Pauline doctrine of the all-sufficiency of faith – an attempt to make the Christian's moral obligations more definite.

So far the so-called 'Doctrina.' The *Didache* itself was probably written some thirty or more years later than the early date suggested for the 'Doctrina' – i.e. about 130. It consists of a developed statement of the Two Ways; most of the above precepts are found, and many others. A few striking examples may be added:

Love those that hate you, and you shall not have an enemy.

Abstain from fleshly and bodily lusts.

To everyone that asketh of thee, give and ask not back, for to all the Father wills that gifts be given from his own bounties. Blessed is he who gives according to the commandment, for he is guiltless.

The accidents that befall thee thou shalt welcome as good, knowing that nothing is done without God.

Resch, whose important work on the agrapha was referred to in a previous chapter, considered that the sentence above – 'for to all the Father wills . . .' – was certainly a genuine saying of Jesus. In addition to this ethical teaching, the *Didache* contains many directions regarding Church order and practice – fasting and prayer, the Lord's Supper, the Lord's Day, and Church officers. Many of these are of considerable interest but they are rather outside the scope of our present study.

(3) *The Epistle of Barnabas* was probably written at about the same time – 130. It also, like various later works, incorporates much of the Two Ways teaching. This is one reason why it is not possible now to regard it as the actual work of the apostle, though of course it is not impossible that some earlier draft of it did come from his hands. It contains a number of strange allegorical interpretations of Old Testament passages but little that refers directly to Christ. The most interesting passages are these:

He preached, teaching Israel and doing such signs and wonders, and loved them intensely. And when he chose his apostles, which were afterwards to publish his gospel, he took men who had been very great sinners, that thereby he might plainly show that he came not to call the righteous but sinners to repentance.

So, since he has renewed us by the forgiveness of sins, he has made us another type, so that we should have the souls of children, as though he were creating us anew.

So he says, Those who wish to see me and lay hold of my kingdom must receive me through tribulation and suffering.

The last of these is also quoted by a later writer in close association with other Gospel texts, and is almost certainly a genuine saying. There is probably a reference to it in Acts 14, 22.

(4) *The Epistles of Ignatius* to various Churches and to Polycarp were written early in the second century when he

was on his way to Rome for trial and martyrdom (115). It is generally agreed that there are seven genuine letters, various others which used to be linked with them being now judged spurious. They contain many references to the facts of the Gospel, warnings against the 'Docetic' heresy (that Jesus only appeared to suffer and died in semblance not reality), and a very developed view of the authority of bishops. There is only one passage that may be considered as adding anything to our knowledge of the Gospel story – a resurrection appearance which differs slightly from the canonical account. It is stated by Jerome to have been found in the 'Gospel according to the Hebrews', and we will consider it when we study that Gospel. There are some fine passages urging meekness and endurance, but nothing to suggest that they are actual agrapha.

(5) *The Epistle of Polycarp to the Philippians* belongs to the same period, having been written not long after Ignatius's departure for Rome. It has one point of interest for us – a passage on ' commensurate judgements' similar to that quoted above from the Epistle of Clement. The way it is introduced and the closing sentence are noticeably different and worth quoting:

He who raised him from the dead will raise us also, if we do his will and live by his commands and love what he loved, refraining from all injustice, covetousness, love of money, evil-speaking, false witness, not returning evil for evil or abuse for abuse, or blow for blow, or curse for curse, but remembering what the Lord said when he taught – Do not judge, so that you may not be judged, forgive and you will be forgiven, have mercy so that you may be shown mercy; with the measure you use men will measure back to you; and blessed are the poor and those who are persecuted for their uprightness, for the kingdom of God belongs to them.

It should be added that Polycarp is an important figure in the Early Church, for he is stated by Irenaeus (182) to have known John and conversed with many who had seen Christ. 'And whatsoever things he had heard from them about the Lord and about his miracles and about his teaching, Polycarp, as having received them from eye-witnesses of the life of the Word, would relate it altogether in accordance with the scriptures.' As he was eighty-six years of age when martyred about the year 156, it seems reasonable to think of him as a very valuable link with the earliest days of the Church. We may wish that he had left us more definite information about them – and in particular, more sayings of Jesus.

(6) *The Expositions of the Sayings of the Lord*, written by Papias in five books, has already been referred to. It is unfortunate that so few fragments of it have come down to us, for Papias was a disciple of John and must surely have recorded many valuable reminiscences of his teaching and that of others with whom he spoke. He was probably born about the same time as Polycarp, who was a friend of his, and his book may be dated about 130. Apart from the passage quoted in a previous chapter about his acquaintance with the followers of the apostles, two statements of his about the composition of the Gospels have been preserved by Eusebius, as follows:

The elder John used to say, Mark having become Peter's interpreter, wrote accurately all that he remembered, though he did not record in order that which was done or said by Christ. For he neither heard the Lord nor followed him, but subsequently as I said attached himself to Peter who used to frame his teaching to meet the wants of his hearers, and not as making a connected narrative of the Lord's discourses. So Mark committed no error, as he wrote down some things just as he recalled them to mind. For he took heed to one thing, to omit none of the facts that he heard and to state nothing falsely in his narrative of them.

Matthew composed the oracles in the Hebrew language, and each one interpreted them as he was able.

Eusebius quotes a number of other statements made by Papias – that the daughters of the apostle Philip told him of one raised from the dead in their time, and Justus Barsabas (Acts 1, 23) drank a deadly poison but received no injury. Also, that Papias recorded a story of a woman accused of many sins before the Lord, which the 'Gospel according to the Hebrews', also contained. We shall consider this last statement in a later chapter.

The only actual passage of teaching ascribed to Jesus in Papias's book is a fantastic account of the corporeal reign of Christ on earth. Eusebius was aware of this but did not quote it, regarding Papias apparently as 'very limited in comprehension'. It is given however by Irenaeus as follows:

The days will come in which vines shall grow, each having ten thousand shoots, and on one shoot ten thousand branches, and on one branch again ten thousand twigs, and on each twig ten thousand clusters, and in each cluster ten thousand grapes, and each grape when pressed shall yield five-and-twenty measures of wine. And when any of the saints shall have taken hold of one of the clusters another shall cry, I am a better cluster, take me, bless the Lord through me. Likewise also a grain of wheat shall produce ten thousand heads, and every head shall have ten thousand grains, and every grain ten pounds of fine flour, bright and clean; and the other fruits, seeds, and the grass shall produce in similar proportions; and all the animals, using these fruits which are products of the soil, shall become in their turn peaceable and harmonious, obedient to man in all subjection. ... And when Judas the traitor believed not and asked, How then shall these growths be accomplished by the Lord? the Lord said, They shall see who shall come thereto.

It has often been thought, as for example by Dr Westcott, one of the chief architects of the Revised New Testament, that some real teaching of Jesus lies behind this fantasy. He certainly taught his disciples to look forward to the time when God's will would be done on earth as in heaven, and certainly the yield of harvest would be vastly increased if ungodliness, ignorance, lust, greed, and war were conquered and cast away.

(7) *The Shepherd of Hermas* is the longest, but from our point of view the least valuable, of these books. It was apparently written round about A.D. 100 at Rome; there is a reference in it to Clement (see above). It is a strange imaginative work, more like the *Pilgrim's Progress* than anything in the Bible. There is however one big difference – there is

a complete absence of actual quotations from the Scriptures. The name Jesus does not occur in it, Christ is found once only, but there are frequent references to the Son, the Lord, and the Holy Spirit. It professes to be the work of an inspired prophet and the claim was often accepted in the early Church – in fact it was very nearly admitted to the canon. It consists of five visions or revelations, twelve mandates or commands, and ten parables – and it is remarkable that Hermas felt entirely free to lay down commands and narrate parables quite different from anything in the Bible. But in spite of this independence and originality, the tone and spirit of it are definitely and sometimes strikingly Christian. Canon Streeter says that 'there is probably no document which reflects better the simplicity and genuine piety of the rank and file of the average church members in the sub-apostolic age.' One example may be given which suggests the value of Hermas to us as a witness to the fact of Christian teaching though not of the actual words of Jesus himself:

Do right, and from your labours which God gives you give generously to all who are in need, not questioning to whom to give or to whom not to give. Give to all, for God wishes that from what he gives gifts should be made to all. So those who receive will account to God as to why they have accepted it and for what purpose.

There are parallels to this in the *Didache* and elsewhere.

(8) Finally, there is the work known as *The Second Epistle of Clement*, which was found in close association with the epistle of Clement already considered but is now generally recognized as quite independent of it. It is often thought to be a sermon or exhortation by Soter who was Bishop of Rome from 166 to 174. Its date is uncertain, but if it belongs to that period it lies outside the limits commonly assigned to the Apostolic Fathers. However, it is convenient to deal with it here because it has for so long been linked with them. Several passages suggest that the writer made use of a variant tradition of Gospel material as well as of the canonical Gospels. The following are of most interest:

For he saith, Not everyone that saith unto me, Lord, Lord, shall be saved, but he that doeth righteousness.

The Lord said, Though ye be gathered together with me in my bosom and do not my commandments, I will cast you away and will say unto you, Depart from me, I know you not whence you are, ye workers of iniquity.

For the Lord said in the Gospel, If ye kept not that which is little who shall give unto you that which is great? For I say unto you that he which is faithful in the least is faithful also in much.

For the Lord saith, Ye shall be as lambs in the midst of wolves. But Peter answering said unto him, What then if the wolves tear the lambs? Jesus said unto Peter, Let not the lambs fear the wolves after they are dead, and ye also fear not them that kill you and are not able to do anything to you ; but fear him who after you are dead hath power over soul and body to cast them into the gehenna of fire.

For the Lord himself being asked by someone when his kingdom should come said, When the two shall be one, and the outside as the inside, and the male with the female neither male nor female.

The first three of these may possibly be just loose misquotations, the fourth sounds more like an alternative recollection of familiar teaching, while the last is definitely a reference to an incident not recorded in the Gospels. Whether it is an authentic reminiscence will be considered later when we come to the 'Gospel according to the Egyptians', which contains several allied passages.

DEFENDERS OF THE FAITH

The books we considered in the previous chapter were written by Christians, to and for Christians, by way of encouragement and exhortation. But it was quite naturally an age of controversy, the Church having to meet the attacks both of pagans and of Jews. We proceed therefore to examine a number of 'Apologies' which have either survived from early days or of which we have information; some of them are in the form of 'Dialogues' between a Christian and a Jew. We are not of course making a study of this apologetic literature, but simply scrutinizing the books that remain to see what help they can give us in our search for knowledge of Jesus beyond the Gospels.

Reference was made in Chapter 3 to a rescript sent by the Emperor Hadrian to Minucius Fundanus, proconsul of Asia, possibly as a result of an Apology presented to him when he visited Athens in 125, the apologist being Quadratus, a Christian philosopher of that city. This work has not survived, but Eusebius has preserved the following interesting extract:

The deeds of our Saviour were always before you, for they were true miracles; those that were healed, those that were raised from the dead, who were seen, not only when healed and when raised, but were always present. They remained living a long time, not only whilst our Lord was on earth, but likewise when he had left the earth. So that some of them have lived also to our own times.

This does not of course mean to the date of the writing of the apology, but merely that Quadratus was a younger contemporary of some aged folk who had seen Jesus – a perfectly possible occurrence. Jairus's daughter might well have lived to 70 or 80, and Quadratus have been a young man when she died. The brevity of this extract is rather tantalizing and makes one wish that the full apology might be discovered, and that is of course a very real possibility as the case of the *Apology* of Aristides shows, to which we now turn.

After quoting the above passage, Eusebius referred to Aristides – 'a faithful man attached to our religion, who also addressed an apology to Hadrian.' This was lost until in the latter part of the nineteenth century an Armenian version of part of it was published by the Lazarist monks of Venice, and a Syriac version was discovered by Dr J. Rendel Harris in the convent of St Catherine on Mt Sinai. Finally, Dr J. Armitage Robinson realized that a Greek version had for a long time been extant, though unrecognized as such. Examination of it convinced Dr Harris that it was a little later in date than had been thought, and that it was addressed not to Hadrian but to his successor Antoninus Pius in the early part of his reign (138–161).

The *Apology* gives a noble picture of the manner of life of the early Church, as well as much argument about the foolishness and futility of pagan beliefs and worship. One or two sentences may be quoted, which show links both with the Gospels and the *Didache*:

Whatever they do not wish that others should do to them they do not practise towards anyone, and they do not eat of the meats of idol sacrifices for they are undefiled, and those that grieve them they comfort and make them their friends, and they do good to their enemies.

They walk in all humility and kindness, and falsehood is not found among them, and they love one another; and from the widows they do not turn away their countenance; and he who has gives to him who has not without grudging.

But the good deeds which they do, they do not proclaim in the ears of the multitude, and they take care that no one shall perceive them, and they hide their gift as he who has found a treasure and hides it.

Dr Harris thinks it is evident from the following passage

that the Church already had a Symbol of the Faith, or formulated creed:

It is said that God came down from heaven and from a Hebrew virgin took and clad himself with flesh, and in a daughter of man there dwelt the Son of God. This is taught from that Gospel which a little while ago was spoken among them as being preached; wherein if ye also will read, ye will comprehend the power that is upon it. This Jesus then was born of the tribe of the Hebrews, and he had twelve disciples in order that a certain dispensation of his might be fulfilled. He was pierced by the Jews; and he died and was buried; and they say that after three days he rose and ascended to heaven; and then these twelve disciples went forth into the known parts of the world, and taught concerning his greatness, with all humility and sobriety.

The Armenian version is more explicit still about the guilt of the Jews – 'he was nailed on the cross by the Jews.' The absence of reference to the Romans is of course what might have been expected in an appeal to the Roman Emperor, but it is interesting to find the apostolic attribution of blame to the Jews (Acts 2, 23; 7, 52; 1 Thess. 2, 15) confirmed in this way.

We come now to Justin Martyr, who was killed at Rome in 165 after a public disputation with a heathen opponent. He wrote two apologies and his famous *Dialogue with Trypho the Jew*. How far this and other dialogues of this kind are to be regarded as authentic narratives is of course a difficult question, but there are good reasons for not just easily ruling them out as entirely fictitious. Dr Emery Barnes speaks of a manuscript which records the trial of the Scillitan martyrs at Carthage about 200 as 'probably preserving the actual shorthand notes taken at the trial'. And as stated earlier there is plenty of other evidence of the use of shorthand in those days.

There are many references to the Gospel story in these three books, and they raise some interesting questions. He speaks of 'the memoirs of the apostles, also called Gospels', and much discussion has taken place as to what he meant by this. After a valuable study of the whole matter Dr

Sanday came to the conclusion that Justin did know and use our Gospels, but that 'he did not assign to them an exclusive authority, and that he probably made use along with them of other documents no longer extant.' Are we perhaps here on the track of one or more of those lost writings to which St Luke's preface refers?

The most interesting 'extra' statements I have found in Justin are these:

When Joseph could find no place in the village where he might lodge, he put up in a cave which was near the village; and when they were there, Mary brought forth the Christ and laid him in a manger, where the Magi, who came from Arabia, found him.

He was used to follow the employment of a carpenter among men, making ploughs and yokes.

John baptized him, when he went down into the water, and a fire was kindled in Jordan.

When he was crucified, they did shoot out the lip, and wagged their heads saying, Let him who raised the dead save himself.

It was not an uncommon thing in the East to have a stable in a cave, so this statement does not necessarily contradict the Gospel account. The fact that Justin was born in Palestine, not very far from Jerusalem, may possibly mean that his statement was based on local knowledge. There are various other references in ancient writings to this point.

As regards agrapha, we have already noticed Christ's warning of 'schisms' and 'factions' in the Church (p. 19). Other passages of interest are as follows:

Be ye kind and merciful, as your Father also is kind and merciful, and maketh his sun to rise on sinners and the righteous and the wicked.

I give unto you power to tread on serpents and scorpions and scolopendras and on all the power of the enemy.

I came not to call the righteous to repentance but sinners, for the Heavenly Father desireth the sinner's repentance rather than his punishment.

Out of which trials he has promised to deliver us and clothe us with prepared garments, if we do his commandments; and he has undertaken to provide an eternal kingdom.

Our Lord urged us by patience and meekness to lead all from shame and the lust of evil.

In whatsoever things I apprehend you, in these I shall judge you.

The last of these sayings is much better attested than many of the agrapha, nearly a score of instances of it being found. It is usually interpreted in some such way as this: 'A renegade cannot plead that he was once a true man; on the other hand, the Lord will not cast it in the teeth of a penitent that he once was an enemy.'

There are a number of later Apologists with whose work we cannot deal here. But there are two dialogues which must be considered because though of late date it seems certain that they are based upon a much earlier and more primitive dialogue not now extant; their citations of Gospel matter show some strange features which may therefore date back to the period we are considering. They are the *Dialogue of Athanasius and Zacchaeus* and the *Dialogue of Timothy and Aquila*, which in their present form both date from the fourth century, but the lost document in the background probably belonged to the second. It is often thought that it was a widely used *Dialogue of Papiscus and Jason* which was actually ascribed by some writers to St Luke and by others to Aristion, mentioned by Papias as one from whom he gleaned information.

The editor of these two documents, F. C. Conybeare, speaks of the 'constant use of an archaic form of Gospel' in the Timothy-Aquila dialogue, which he thinks better preserves the common basis than the other. He instances particularly the reference to the Entry into Jerusalem and what followed. Branches of olive trees are mentioned, and the elders as well as the priests criticize what the disciples are shouting, their comment taking an unusual form, 'Dost thou not hear what these witness against thee?' Immediately following the Entry, Jesus tells the parable of the

Vineyard, which in the Gospels is separated from it by several paragraphs, and there is a strange harmonizing of the Gospel accounts. Finally, there is a definite statement that when Jesus was on trial the only thing he said was 'Behold, your house is left desolate' – words which of course are found at an earlier stage of the story in the Gospels.

In the Athanasius-Zacchaeus dialogue there is an odd passage where Mary and Elizabeth are spoken of as meeting in Jerusalem before their children are born, which seems to contradict Luke 1, 39 – 'a city of Juda'. And the birth of Jesus is actually stated to have taken place in Jerusalem, he being taken to Bethlehem subsequently. Immediately after his birth he caused the star to appear in the heaven and the Magi to start from Arabia! All this sounds much more apocryphal than the Timothy-Aquila passage just discussed, where it does appear that we may be touching some very primitive material. Like Justin, the writer speaks of the 'memoirs of the apostles'.

One other little book must be mentioned here, though it really contains nothing of value for our study. It is the *Epistle to Diognetus*, which is often included amongst the Apostolic Fathers, but is really an 'apology', differing however from those already considered, 'in that it was written not to conciliate an enemy but to satisfy an enquirer,' as one writer puts it. Who the writer was is unknown, nor is it certain who Diognetus was, though it has often been thought that the reference is to a tutor of Marcus Aurelius who was so named. That would give us somewhere in the middle of the second century as the date of writing. The Epistle gives an attractive picture of the life of Christian people in those days, similar to that in the *Apology of Aristides*, and it adds the rather striking thought that 'what the soul is to the body, Christians are to the world'. In a passage on the coming of Christ it says:

Him sent he to them. Was it then, as human reckoning might have it, in despotism and fear and terror? No indeed, but in gentleness and meekness, as a king he sent his kingly son. He sent him as God sent him as man to men. As saving he sent, as persuading and not to force. For force does not belong to God. As calling he sent, not pursuing. As loving he sent, not judging.

It is interesting to find, here again as elsewhere, emphasis upon the humility and gentleness of Christ, and of such qualities as these having become the characteristic way of life of his followers.

CHAPTER 12

THE APOCRYPHAL GOSPELS

IN view of the statement at the beginning of Luke's Gospel that many writers had undertaken 'to set forth in order a declaration of those things which are most surely believed among us', it is natural that such a study as that on which we are now engaged should include an investigation into the possibility that some of these other books may have survived wholly or in part. And the well-known fact that there are certain 'apocryphal Gospels' extant suggests that we have in them material for this enquiry. But in point of fact that is hardly so.

The word 'apocryphal' has had an odd history, and has been used in three different ways. It properly means 'secret', and it was originally applied to certain Jewish and Christian books which were supposed to contain hidden teaching, too sacred for ordinary people to possess; they were often ascribed, quite fictitiously, to ancient worthies – patriarchs, prophets, or apostles. Gradually as the falsity of these ascriptions was recognized the word came to acquire a new significance – 'spurious' – and lists of such books were drawn up with the intention that they should be excluded from use, especially in public worship. To these two meanings a third was added in the sixteenth century when the Reformers applied it to those books, subsidiary to the Old Testament, which were found in the Greek and Latin versions but not in the Hebrew – the books of Wisdom, Maccabees, and others. They were regarded by the Roman Church as part of the Old Testament, but the Reformers relegated them to a secondary position and named them the 'Old Testament Apocrypha'. They have often been bound up in our Bibles between the Testaments and regarded as

Scripture, though on a rather lower level of value. They are not secret or spurious but secondary.

Now it is in this third sense that the word was employed by William Hone in the title of his book *The Apocryphal New Testament*, first published in 1820 but reprinted many times since. It contained a number of supposed Gospels and Epistles and other books, arranged with headings and chapters and verses as in the Bible, the suggestion clearly being that it was a supplementary collection of early Christian material – a kind of New Testament parallel to the Old Testament Apocrypha. Hone actually stated in his preface that it contained 'the writings which were not included in the New Testament by its compilers when it was first collected into a volume.' This gives an utterly misleading idea of the formation of the canon, as though there was an arbitrary selection of books at some particular date, these others being left on one side. The truth of course is that the good sense of the Church through a process of years gradually determined which books were of supreme value. Moreover, Hone's own selection of books was a completely arbitrary one – there being vastly more of the sort he included than those he chose.

A modern book with the same title was published in 1924 by Dr M. R. James, Provost of Eton, but he used the word 'apocryphal' not in Hone's sense of supplementary or secondary but in its earlier (though not original) sense of false and spurious. He violently criticized Hone's book, speaking of it as 'a very bad book' and quite misleading – for the reason I have outlined above. He confessed that it had exercised a fascination upon him years before as it first introduced him to this whole subject, but he deliberately prepared his own volume as a corrective. In it he gathered an immense number of Gospels, Epistles, Acts, and Apocalypses, written in Greek and Latin, Syriac and Coptic. He was not however quite consistent in his use of the word 'apocryphal', for though the bulk of the material is of the false and fictitious type, yet he included also the fragments of what we may call secondary Gospels – those which seem to have some relation to the canonical Gospels and have been thought to incorporate some primitive elements.

Now as regards the conventionally called 'apocryphal Gospels', both those printed by Hone and the much larger number in James's book, it does not take very much examination to convince us that they are almost entirely fiction not fact. They deal mostly with the nativity and boyhood of Jesus on the one hand, and with his passion and resurrection on the other. Many fantastic miracles are attributed to the child Jesus, as for example that he made birds of clay and then they flew away, and again that another boy who accidentally ran against him dropped down and died. We need not spend time on these matters. Preachers have often referred to such stories to point the contrast between them and the spirit of our Gospels – a kind of negative argument for the historical accuracy of the latter.

But we cannot rule out the possibility that here and there some small points of authentic tradition may have survived amidst all the fiction and fantasy. Readers of Gibbon's *Decline and Fall of the Roman Empire* will remember that he quotes from Eusebius, the Church historian of the fourth century, the story that the grandsons of Jude, the brother of Jesus, were examined by the Emperor Domitian and that they were still alive in the time of Trajan (A.D. 98–117). It is clearly not impossible if that really happened that some family names and narratives may have been handed down into the second century. Bishop Ellicott considered that the names given in one of these books for the parents of Mary – Joachim and Anna – might probably be relied upon. And Dean Farrar in his *Life of Christ* quoted the following charming little tale and thought it might be based on fact:

Now in the month of Adar, Jesus assembled the boys as if he were their king; they strewed their garments on the ground and he sat upon them. Then they put on his head a crown wreathed of flowers and like attendants waiting on a king they stood in order before him on his right hand and on his left. And whoever passed that way the boys took him by force saying, Come hither and adore the King and then proceed upon thy way.

This is quite different from the usual grotesque narratives, and is something that might quite easily have happened – and been remembered and retold. But it cannot be more than an interesting possibility. We are reminded of the beautiful little Russian carol 'When Jesus Christ was yet a child', translated by Geoffrey Dearmer, with music by Tschaikovsky. It is probably based on this story.

Many of these Gospels are heretical – that is, they were deliberately written in support of ideas and teachings other than those of the orthodox Church. For example, the 'Gospel of Peter' is a product of Docetism, the view that the body of Jesus was not real but only *seemed* to be so (that is the meaning of the term) and that therefore his sufferings were only apparent not actual. It is also very anti-Jewish in its sentiment. It was written about 150, and was one of the earliest apocryphal writings. Eusebius tells us that it was accustomed to be read in the church at Rhossus near Antioch but was suppressed by Serapion, the Bishop of Antioch, when he found on examination its heretical tendency. This gives an interesting hint of how in those early times people felt free to modify traditional statements and teaching, or even to create new narratives in support of views about which they had come to feel strongly. It is not easy for us with our entirely different standards of literary ethics to sympathize with their attitude, but it is important to realize that this was their standard then, for it explains much of this apocryphal literature. Long post-resurrection teaching was often put into the mouth of Jesus without any historical justification. It is obviously very unlikely that any historical elements will be found here to supplement the knowledge of Jesus that the canonical Gospels give us.

There is however one point of a general nature that may be made. It is surely a remarkable testimony to the impact that the personality of Jesus made upon the first generations of Christians that such an enormous literature should grow up concerning him, and also that the exploits of his apostles in the early days of the expansion of the Church should have been so impressive and fascinating that such a luxuriant growth of imagination and legend should result. A lesser Man – and lesser men – would not have produced such an amazing harvest. There is something of the same kind in the case of Mohammed and of St Francis, but not on anything like the same scale. The growth of saga is an interesting and often an astonishing thing, but in this case it does seem to bear witness to the reality and the greatness of the Figure in the background who has so wonderfully gripped the imagination of mankind.

We come now to the question of secondary Gospels, apocryphal only in the sense of being uncanonical and supplementary. Only fragments remain, and in some cases if they were extant in full we might have to group them with the heretical writings. But there do appear to have been several comparatively early Gospels which were referred to with respect by certain of the Fathers and which may quite probably have contained some primitive material. It does not seem likely, however, that any of those spoken of by Luke have so far been discovered.

The most important of these is the 'Gospel according to the Hebrews', to which we will devote our next chapter. We shall consider there the question whether there were several different Gospels in use amongst Jewish Christians or whether various other names all refer to the same Gospel – the 'Gospel of the Nazarenes', the 'Gospel of the Twelve', the 'Ebionite Gospel'. It is rather an involved business, but we shall concentrate attention on the interesting passages that remain, some of which seem to be of real value.

Next in importance is the 'Gospel according to the Egyptians', to which Clement of Alexandria (A.D. 200) refers on several occasions. It apparently included a strange conversation between Jesus and a certain Salome on the question of marriage; the evidence points to this having been amended by the Encratites, who abstained from marriage, but that originally it did not imply this. In its simplest form it probably read thus, or nearly so:

After the Word had told about the End, Salome said, How long shall death prevail? And the Lord made answer, So long as women bear children.

And when Salome said, I have done well then in not bearing children? the Lord answered and said, Every plant eat thou, but that which hath bitterness eat not.

When Salome enquired when the things concerning which she asked should be known, the Lord said, When ye have trampled on the garment of shame, and when the two become one, and the male with the female is neither male nor female.

There are several alternative versions of these sayings, and it seems probable that we have primitive and quite possibly genuine material intermingled with heretical, but that it is not possible to be quite sure how to sift the grain from the chaff. In particular, I am inclined to think that the saying quoted in a previous chapter from the so-called 'Second Epistle of Clement' is really a more original form of the last of the above passages:

For the Lord himself being asked by someone when his kingdom should come said, When the two shall be one, and the outside as the inside, and the male with the female neither male nor female.

Bishop Lightfoot studied these passages at some length and came to the conclusion that no condemnation of marriage is implied in the original form of them, and that quite possibly a real incident lies in the background. He suggested that the last one really amounts to a call to mutual harmony, perfect sincerity, and the conquest of sensual passion. The touch of enigma about the sayings is of course paralleled in various texts in the Gospels; I believe that Jesus sometimes deliberately framed his teaching in puzzling form to arouse curiosity and to stimulate thought.

Finally, we must just notice that in recent years there have been unearthed in Egypt quite a number of fragments of papyrus on which are written Gospel material. Some of these are 'Sayings of Jesus' perhaps culled from various sources, but others are definitely portions of lost Gospels. We shall study all these in a later chapter, but they must be mentioned here because some of them may belong to one or other of the uncanonical Gospels we have been considering.

CHAPTER 13

THE HEBREW GOSPEL

━━

QUITE a number of Church writers from the second to the fourth century refer to and quote from a Gospel written in Hebrew and used amongst different groups of Jewish Christians. Both Clement of Alexandria and Origen did so, evidently regarding it as worth using though not on a level with the Four. Eusebius states that Hegesippus used it (175), and that the Ebionites used it alone. Epiphanius speaks of the Nazarenes having the Gospel according to Matthew quite complete in Hebrew, but that the Ebionites used a mutilated form of it. Jerome has many more references and says that he was allowed to copy it by the Nazarenes of Beroea in Syria and that he translated it into Greek and Latin.

Doubts have been expressed whether all these and various other statements all refer to the same document, or whether two or more were involved. We cannot enter into this argument here, but my own conviction as argued at length elsewhere * is that there was one such Gospel only, though different editions or copies of it may have varied somewhat. In particular it seems probable that the Ebionites, an ascetic group of Jewish Christians, had their own recension of it.

There is also complete uncertainty about the origin of the Gospel and its connexion with the Synoptic Gospels, for it is evidently much more akin to them – to Matthew especially – than are any of the apocryphal books we considered in the last chapter. It has most generally been thought to have been a rewritten Matthew, amplified by fanciful embellishments and so forth. But there are difficulties about this; in an ancient stichometry, or enumeration of lines in various books, it is stated to have been distinctly shorter than Matthew. And some of its variations or additions have a definitely

* *The Expository Times*, July and August, 1928.

original and authentic tone about them. It seems more probable therefore that it was a sort of 'first cousin' to Matthew, i.e. a different compilation from some of the sources of Matthew with other additional material. We cannot deal here with the various possible ways in which this may have come about. My own view is outlined in the articles mentioned above.

But whatever view of these points is held it certainly seems probable that this Hebrew Gospel, more than any of the other uncanonical Gospels, may have extra information to give us regarding Jesus – which makes one wonder why it has not survived to the present day, especially in view of the fact that there are traces of it being extant in the Middle Ages. In certain Gospel manuscripts dating from the ninth or tenth century there are some marginal notes which give readings from 'the Jewish', and one of these agrees with matter cited by Jerome as in the Hebrew Gospel. Dr James, in the book referred to in the last chapter, calls attention to a quotation from 'the Gospel of the Nazarenes' in a commentary by Haimo of Auxerre (850), and also to a marginal note of the thirteenth century citing it on a copy of the versified Bible called the 'Aurora' in the Fitzwilliam Museum at Cambridge. Many years ago Dr Rendel Harris expressed surprise that 'it has eluded us so long'. The recent discoveries at Qumran and elsewhere arouse an expectation and a hope that we may not have to wait very much longer for it to be unearthed from the sands of Egypt or the caves of Palestine, or maybe from some remote monastery library or lumber room.

We now proceed to examine the principal excerpts from this Gospel that have come down to us.

(1) Behold, the mother of the Lord and his brethren said unto him, John the Baptist baptizeth unto the remission of sins: let us go and be baptized by him. But he said unto them, Wherein have I sinned that I should go and be baptized by him? Unless perhaps this very thing that I have said is ignorance.

This reads to me like a real reminiscence of the brothers of

Jesus (cf. John 7, 3f.). It is natural to suppose that such a suggestion would be made to him and recalled by them later on when their unbelief had passed (Acts 1, 14). Harnack, the famous Church historian, spoke of it as 'the most ancient preliminary history of the baptism that we know', and thought that its ambiguity as to whether or not Jesus was conscious of his own sinlessness was a sign of genuineness. I would add that his words here seem to me to suit exactly what we may feel was his spiritual condition at this time. If we think of him as having hitherto lived a stainless life and come gradually to the conviction that God was calling him to service in some way or other, but that he had not yet that full realization of his person and purpose which the Gospels suggest came to him at the baptism, then the hesitation and uncertainty in this saying appear to be psychologically correct. I regard it as an authentic and illuminating word.

(2) And it came to pass when the Lord had come up from the water the entire fountain of the Holy Spirit descended and rested upon him, and said unto him, My son, in all the prophets did I await thee, that thou mightest come and I might rest in thee. For thou art my rest – thou art my first-born son, that reignest for ever.

We should notice the words 'said *unto him*', for there is no such explicit statement in the Gospels that the voice was *to* him and *for* him, not the bystanders. Dr Menzies has given its significance well in this way, 'Here more distinctly than in any of the canonical Gospels the baptism is the act by which Jesus is made acquainted with his destiny to bring about the highest revelation of God.'

It must always be remembered that it is almost certainly due to Jesus himself that we have any account of the baptism at all – we are reading his spiritual autobiography, so to speak. It is surely quite credible then that he would tell his disciples of this great crisis on more than one occasion, and not in exactly the same form of words. Actually there is still another version found in the Ebionite Gospel which we will notice presently. May not these variant accounts all be but partially successful attempts to declare the wonder of the en-

lightenment which came to him and the rise into his consciousness of the conviction of his messianic vocation?

(3) Just now my mother the Holy Spirit took me by one of my
hairs and carried me off to the great mountain Tabor.

This odd saying is quoted several times, both by Origen and
by Jerome. It is generally supposed to refer to the story of
the temptation, and the description of the Holy Spirit as 'my
mother' is explained by the fact that the Hebrew word for
spirit is feminine. I have offered a different interpretation
which I find attractive though it has not won much support.
It is that the words 'my mother' do not refer to 'the Holy
Spirit' but are vocative, i.e. Jesus is addressing his mother.
Read thus it would appear to be a boyish remark made by
him, telling perhaps of a long walk and an experience of
spiritual blessing.

(4) If thy brother, he saith, have sinned in word and given
thee satisfaction, seven times in a day receive him. Simon his disciple said unto him, Seven times in a day? The Lord answered and
said unto him, Yea, I say unto thee, unto seventy times seven. For
with the prophets also after they were anointed with the Holy
Spirit, there was found sinful speech.

Dr Burkitt considered that this passage bore all the marks of
superior originality to the parallels in the canonical Gospels.
The unusual statement about the prophets is very remarkable, indicating a free and untraditional attitude to the old
Scriptures. It is difficult if not impossible to think of a later
writer fabricating it, especially one who included such references to the prophets as the last two passages. That they
were anointed with the Holy Spirit is of course a familiar
thought (Isaiah 61, 1, etc.), but many passages in their
books are sufficient to demonstrate the truth of the observa-
tion attributed here to Jesus. The little Book of Obadiah, for
example, is in effect a 'hymn of hate' directed against Edom.

(5) The other of the rich men said unto him, Master, what good
thing shall I do to live? He said to him, Man, do the law and the
prophets. He answered him, I have. He said to him, Go, sell all

that thou hast, and distribute to the poor, and come follow me. But the rich man began to scratch his head, and it pleased him not. And the Lord said unto him, How sayest thou, I have done the law and the prophets, since it is written in the law, Thou shalt love thy neighbour as thyself, and behold many brethren of thine, sons of Abraham, are clad in filth, dying of hunger, and thy house is full of good things, and nothing at all goes out from it to them? And he turned and said to Simon his disciple, who was sitting by him, Simon son of John, it is easier for a camel to enter through the eye of a needle than for a rich man to enter into the kingdom of heaven.

While a few writers have regarded this as a more primitive version of the familiar story, chiefly because of its several realistic touches, the more usual estimate is that it is dependent on the Synoptic narrative and distinctly secondary. It has been argued that the story was re-told thus in order to mitigate the severity of Christ's words by showing that the man had been living a selfish life, whereas in the Gospels the point is simply that at this particular crisis he refused to sacrifice.

But the point has commonly been missed that the story is told here not as a different version of the familiar incident but as a different though similar event. 'The *other* of the rich men' makes that clear, as does the reference to Simon and to his sitting posture, for in the Gospels it happened when they were on the road. It may of course be thought strange that two happenings of the same sort should occur, but it is by no means impossible. If, on the other hand, it is an alternative account then it certainly does appear to have certain primitive touches which it is worth preserving.

(6) And when the Lord had given his linen cloth to the servant of the priest, he went to James and appeared unto him. For James had sworn that he would not eat bread from that hour wherein the Lord had drunk the cup until he saw him rising from the dead. Bring a table and bread, saith the Lord. He took up the bread and blessed and broke, and afterwards gave to James the Just, and said to him, My brother, eat thy bread, for the Son of man is risen from them that sleep.

That Jesus appeared to James is of course stated by St Paul, as we have noticed earlier (1 Cor. 15, 7), and many scholars have considered this account of what happened as substantially accurate, though no doubt with embellishing touches. An obscure point is the reference to the 'servant of the priest', but on the other hand the use of the phrase 'the Son of man' has an authentic sound about it; commonly used in the New Testament only by Jesus himself, its presence here is noteworthy. James and the other brothers of Jesus did not at first believe in or follow him (Mark 3, 31; John 7, 5), but they were amongst the disciples after the crucifixion (Acts 1, 14). This story appears to give the clue to their change of attitude.

(7) And when he came to Peter and those about him he said to them, Take, feel me, and see that I am not a bodiless devil. And straightway they touched him and believed.

This statement is found in one of the letters of Ignatius, who was martyred in 115, and Jerome later on stated that it was found in the Hebrew Gospel. If this is accurate it gives an early date for this Gospel. It is no doubt an alternative account of the appearance narrated in Luke 24, 36–39, but the expression 'bodiless devil' is interesting, reminding us that the disciples were frightened because they thought it was an appearance boding evil. It is possible that this is an earlier account than that in Luke as it is the more difficult of the two expressions, and it would be quite in the manner of that Gospel to soften down a rather harsh word.

(8) Never rejoice, except when you have looked upon your brother in love.

(9) It is said that this Gospel placed among the greatest sins if a man have grieved the spirit of his brother.

(10) I will select to myself the good, those good ones whom my Father in heaven has given me.

(11) He shall not cease from seeking until he find, and having found he will be amazed, and having been amazed will reign, and having reigned will rest.

These four sayings have all been thought genuine by many

scholars. The first two breathe the very spirit of Christian brotherliness, stressing the inwardness of true love. The third sounds rather cryptic, but may mean that those who become good by God's grace he will select for finer service. The last is also found amongst the papyrus 'Sayings of Jesus', as we shall notice in a later chapter.

(12) This Gospel had an interesting variant version of the parable of the talents. It 'turned the threat not against the man who hid the talent, but against him who had lived riotously – for it told of three servants, one who devoured his master's substance with harlots and flute-girls, another who multiplied it by trading, and another who hid the talent; and made the one to be accepted, another only rebuked, and another to be shut up in prison.'

The two canonical versions of this parable vary considerably (Matt. 25; Luke 19), and Jesus may well have taught a third variant – like all teachers he no doubt repeated his teaching but modified it according to circumstances and occasions.

These are the principal passages quoted from the Hebrew Gospel, but some smaller points may be added. The man whose hand was withered is said to have appealed thus for help, 'I was a mason, seeking a livelihood with my hands; I pray thee, Jesus, restore to me health, that I may not shamefully beg my food.' In the Lord's Prayer it had 'Our bread *of the morrow* give us this day.' It contained a story of a woman accused of many sins – probably a variant of the narrative in John 7, 53–8, 11; we shall return to this point in a later chapter. Regarding Christ's intercession on the cross this Gospel said 'At this word of the Lord, many thousands of Jews that stood round about the cross believed.' At the cleansing of the temple, 'rays issued from his eyes whereby they were terrified and put to flight.' Instead of the statement that the veil of the temple was rent we read that a lintel of great size fell and was broken. There are also some minor variations in language recorded in certain Gospel manuscripts with which we cannot deal here. Altogether it seems clear that the Gospel was worthy of the respect which

Origen and others gave it, though we cannot yet exactly assess its worth.

Whether the Ebionites used their own amended version of this Gospel or whether they had something quite different must at present remain uncertain. Two passages quoted from it by Epiphanius (in the fourth century) show no heretical tendency and might quite possibly be also part of the Hebrew Gospel:

It came to pass in the days of Herod the king of Judaea that there came John baptizing with the baptism of repentance in the river Jordan, who was said to be of the lineage of Aaron the priest, child of Zacharias and Elizabeth, and all went out to him.

There was a certain man named Jesus and he was about thirty years old, who chose us. And coming into Capernaum, he entered into the house of Simon who was surnamed Peter, and opened his mouth and said, As I passed by the lake of Tiberias, I chose John and James the sons of Zebedee, and Simon and Andrew, and Thaddeus, and Simon the Zealot and Judas the Iscariot; and thee Matthew, as thou satest at the receipt of custom, I called and thou followedst me. You therefore I will to be twelve apostles for a testimony unto Israel.

Next we have another variant account of the baptism of Jesus and the voice then heard; we shall see in a later chapter that there is other evidence for this version of the story.

After the people were baptized, Jesus also came and was baptized by John; and as he came up from the water the heavens were opened and he saw the Holy Ghost in the likeness of a dove that descended and entered into him, and a voice from heaven saying, Thou art my beloved Son, in thee I am well pleased, and again, This day have I begotten thee. And straightway there shone about the place a great light. Which when John saw he said unto him, Who art thou, Lord? and again there was a voice from heaven saying unto him, This is my beloved Son in whom I am well pleased. And then John fell down before him and said, I beseech thee, Lord, baptize thou me. But he prevented him saying, Suffer it, for thus it behoveth that all things should be fulfilled.

Finally, there are three points where the Ebionite objection to meat food is clearly responsible for variations in the narrative:

And John had raiment of camel's hair and a leathern girdle about his loins; and his meat was wild honey, whereof the taste is that of manna, as a cake in oil.

There is a play on words here, for locust in Greek is 'akris' while cake is 'enkris'.

I came to destroy the sacrifices, and if ye cease not from sacrificing the wrath will not cease from you.

Have I with desire desired to eat this flesh of the Passover with you?

This Gospel then, like the Hebrew Gospel and whatever its relation to it, appears to have some interesting features, and even possibly some primitive traditions intermingled with some more tendentious matter.

A note must be added about the 'Toldoth Yeshu' – the mediaeval Jewish life of Christ which was used for propaganda against the Church. It tells the Talmud illegitimacy story of the birth of Jesus, borrows the clay birds tale from the apocryphal Gospels, and has many other fantastic features. The strangest is the appearance of a Queen Helene amongst the rulers of Palestine before whom Jesus was tried. We cannot go into all this here, but our reason for referring to it at all is that some years ago a book appeared by Hugh J. Schonfield entitled *According to the Hebrews* in which he endeavoured to show that the 'Toldoth' was closely related to the secondary Gospel which we have been studying. He believed that, stripped of the legendary matter that had grown around it, it was of comparatively early date and was indeed a Jewish counterblast or reply to the Hebrew Gospel, based upon it and so quite possibly retaining some hints of what it contained. This theory seems to me to tumble down on the simple fact that the contacts between the 'Toldoth' and the thirty or more extracts we have of the lost Gospel are very few and slight. At the same time there are some puzzling features about this book; it is not at all clear why such teaching as this should have been included, for example, depicting noble aspects of Christian character:

If one of them compel you to go a mile, go with him twain; if a Jew smite you on the left side turn to him the right also; if a Jew revile you, endure it and return it not again, as Yeshu endured it; in meekness he showed himself, therewith he showed you also meekness as he practised it, that ye might endure all that any should do to you. At the last judgement Yeshu will punish them, but do ye have hope according to your meekness, for so it is written, Seek ye the Lord, all ye meek of the earth which have wrought his judgement; seek righteousness, seek meekness, it may be ye shall be hid in the day of the Lord's anger.

We cannot of course be sure that this and some other passages are not Christian interpolations, for there are few manuscripts of it earlier than the sixteenth century, I understand.

CHAPTER 14

MISCELLANEOUS SAYINGS

WE have considered a number of agrapha – from early Church writers, from the Hebrew Gospel, and elsewhere. We come now to those found in various books dating from the end of the second century to the fourth and fifth. It will not be possible to deal much with these books and their writers, and the sources from which they drew these sayings are for the most part unknown. It is of course very possible that some of them came from some of those earlier books we have noticed, the Hebrew Gospel or Papias's *Expositions*.

There are several points about some of these sayings that predispose us to think they may be genuine utterances of Jesus, but of course certainty is impossible. Some of them are framed in figurative and picturesque language as so much is in the Gospels; and there is an enigmatic or cryptic quality about a few which reminds us of such passages as the 'eye of a needle' text (Mark 10, 25); there is also a terseness and aptness very characteristic of Jesus's mode of speech; and there are a number of references to the 'kingdom', which was of course a favourite thought and word of his.

(1) Be wise bankers (or money-changers).

This is the most widely-quoted of the agrapha, Resch enumerating no fewer than sixty-nine instances of it. It is usually found with the familiar words of 1 Thess. 5, 21 attached – 'Be wise bankers, proving all things, holding fast that which is good.' It may therefore quite probably be one of those sayings, to which reference was made in Chapter 2, which were known to and used by Paul. One ancient writer, after quoting the saying, adds 'discerning the genuine coin of the

Lord from the forgery', and another uses it to suggest that there are true and false things in Scripture and that we are to discriminate.

(2) Ask for the great things and the small shall be added to you; ask for the heavenly and the earthly shall be added to you.

Clement of Alexandria (190–200) and Origen (230–250), two of the most famous of the Church scholars in early days, quoted this saying – Clement the first part only, Origen the whole on several occasions. It is closely linked by Clement with Matt. 6, 33 – 'Seek ye first the kingdom of God and his righteousness, and all these things shall be added unto you' – and it has sometimes been thought to be merely a paraphrase of that. But the parallelism is very striking and reminds us of various Gospel texts where this familiar Hebrew literary device is used. It is certainly a fine statement of the faith that if first things are put first, other necessities will not be lacking.

(3) He who is near me is near the fire; he who is far from me is far from the kingdom.

Origen is again the chief authority for this, and the way he introduces it is interesting: 'I have read somewhere what purports to be an utterance of the Saviour, and I query (equally if someone put it into the mouth of the Saviour or if someone remembered it) whether this is true which is said. But the Saviour himself saith....' The parallelism is again striking – this time of the antithetic or contrasted kind. The thought is of the fiery trial of persecution (1 Peter 4, 12), and there may be an allusion to it in the words of Ignatius when on the way to martyrdom at Rome: 'Why have I surrendered myself to death, to fire, to the sword, to the wild beasts? But he who is near to the sword is near to God, he that is among the wild beasts is in company with God.' This saying goes a step further, implying that refusal of the suffering means missing the joy of the kingdom. An alternative form in one writer has 'life' instead of 'kingdom', but the meaning is the same.

(4) Accept not anything from any man, and possess not anything in this world.

This is found in an old Syriac book called *The Doctrine of Addai* which purports to be an account of the visit to Edessa of one of the 'Seventy' (Luke 10, 1), and the founding of the Church there. It consists chiefly of legendary matter (see a reference to it in Chapter 19), but there is reason to think that it was based on fact, and it is quite possible that a true saying might survive in it – especially one that by its enigmatic character could so easily be misunderstood and disliked. For of course there is exaggeration here, as so often in the Gospels. Jesus himself accepted hospitality freely and frequently, and he allowed women to minister to his needs (Luke 8, 2, 3). But he was very outspoken against greed and hoarding, as though life consisted in the abundance of one's possessions, and there seems an echo of this saying in the description of the early Church's brotherly conduct, 'Not one of them said that aught of the things which he possessed was his own' (Acts 4, 32).

(5) That which is weak shall be saved through that which is strong.

This beautiful little saying is commonly thought to be a genuine word of Jesus. It comes from a book called the *Apostolic Church Order* which is based in part on the *Didache*, which we discussed in Chapter 10, but is introduced there in a very curious way – no doubt quite legendary. The apostles are depicted as considering the ordinances of the Church, and John says, 'Ye have forgotten, brethren, when the Teacher asked for the bread and the cup, and blessed them, that he permitted not these (women) to be with us. Martha said, It was because of Mary, because he saw her smiling. Mary said, I did not verily laugh, but I remembered the words of our Lord and was glad, for ye know that he said unto us aforetime when he taught. . . .'

(6) No man that is not tempted shall obtain the kingdom of heaven.

This comes from several writers but in particular from Tertullian (about 200), who includes it in a reference to the Gethsemane story: 'The disciples were tempted because they fell asleep, so that they forsook the Lord when he was taken, and even he who abode with him and used the sword, so that he even denied thrice; for the saying had gone before....' It seems likely that Tertullian had some variant form of the story before him, because he quotes the warning of Jesus in this way, 'Watch and pray, lest ye *fall* into temptation.' The canonical word is of course 'enter', but 'fall' gives the sense of sudden unanticipated encounter which the story really seems to need.

(7) Good things must come, and blessed is he through whom they come. Likewise also evil things must come, and woe to him through whom they come.

The second half of this is of course similar to Matt. 18, 7, but the perfect parallelism here encourages the idea that it is an authentic saying. It comes from the *Clementine Homilies*, one of several books wrongly attributed to Clement of Rome, which however seems to have retained some early and interesting variants of Gospel teaching. The 'bankers' passage, for example, is quoted half a dozen times. And the warning of Jesus about disruption in the family (Matt. 10, 35; Luke 12, 35) appears three times with the significant addition 'brother from brother'.

(8) Except ye make the right hand as the left hand, and the left hand as the right hand, and that which is upwards as that which is downwards, that which is before as that which is behind, ye shall not know the kingdom of God.

That Jesus often spoke in enigmas to arrest attention and arouse thought seems certain from the Gospels, and this is a striking example of that method of teaching. It is an earnest call to repentance and a reversal of old standards; the Greek word for repentance means literally 'change of mind', and it would be difficult to find a more vivid and valuable picture of repentance than this agraphon. When I turn right about face my left hand is where my right hand was, and so on. It is parallel to the familiar text, Matt. 18, 3 – 'Except ye turn and become as little children, ye shall not enter into the kingdom of heaven.' It may be added that there are several other slightly different forms of this saying – this one is from the apocryphal 'Acts of Peter' which is dated by Dr M. R. James as not later than 200. So we are still dealing with comparatively early material.

(9) Because of the signs which he did, they loved the Lord. But the Lord said to them, Why marvel ye at the signs? I give unto you a great inheritance which the whole world hath not.

This and the following saying are from the Homilies of Macarius (fourth century), and we have no clue as to what earlier writing he may have quoted from. The word 'inheritance' does not occur in the Gospels in this sense, but is fairly frequent in the epistles; it would help to explain their use of it if Jesus himself so spoke, but it is of course quite uncertain.

(10) Hear the Lord when he says, Take heed to faith and hope, through which is engendered love towards God and man, which gives eternal life.

There are about a dozen places in the New Testament where these 'three theological virtues', as they are called, are grouped together, and it is certainly an attractive idea that this link was forged by Jesus himself. Resch regarded this saying as a 'master-word' on which all the canonical instances depended, but other scholars disagreed and rejected the saying. Macarius is stated to have 'belonged to the sect of Messalians or Prayermen, who were widespread in Eastern lands, and probably a survival of an early Christian movement.'

(11) But that he was distressed agrees with what he said, How long shall I be with you and speak with you? And in another place, I am weary of this generation. They proved me, he said, ten times, but these twenty times and ten times ten times.

This is found in a Commentary on the Gospels by Ephraem, a famous Syrian scholar, towards the end of the fourth century. It occurs in an exposition of the story of the raising of Lazarus and the distress of Jesus at the tomb, but there is nothing like it in the Gospel at that place (John 11, 33–38). It reminds us of words of Jesus in Mark 9, 19, and of several passages in the Old Testament. It certainly expresses very forcibly the intensity of the emotion Jesus felt as a result of the refusal of his message. But of course it may be just a case of loose quotation or paraphrase.

(12) So when the Lord was telling the disciples about the coming kingdom of the saints, how glorious and marvellous it was, Judas amazed at what was spoken said, And who then shall see these things? And the Lord replied, These things shall they see who become worthy.

This is stated by Hippolytus, an eminent scholar at Rome in the first quarter of the third century. It is noteworthy as including the name of one of the disciples – a very rare occurrence in the agrapha. We have already noticed that Irenaeus quoted a similar statement from Papias (see p. 85); Judas is there described as 'the traitor', and there is no reference to 'becoming worthy', so the two versions of the conversation may be independent of each other – variant recollections perhaps of what some earlier writer had said.

(13) We remember our Lord and Teacher, how he charged us saying, Ye shall keep my secrets (mysteries) for me and the sons of my house.

This is another quotation from the *Clementine Homilies* but with support from Clement of Alexandria and other writers. Clement speaks of it as found 'in a certain Gospel'. It seems like a concise statement of Christ's teaching about 'the mystery of the kingdom of God' (Mark 4, 11), which really means that the principle of spiritual selection is always at work – those who fit themselves by obedience to become sons of God are chosen for higher privileges of fellowship and service.

(14) He himself instructing and warning us in the epistle of John his disciple, Ye see me in yourselves, as one of you sees himself in water or in a mirror.

This strange saying is found in a book, wrongly ascribed to Cyprian, which is said to belong to the oldest literature of the Latin Church. There is nothing like this in the canonical epistles of John, and it is possibly a confused reference to words in the apocryphal Acts of John – 'I am a mirror, to thee who perceivest me.' If that is so, the idea of it being an actual word of Jesus does not arise, as it is one of many parallel expressions in a strange Gnostic hymn. (This was, by the way, set to music by Gustav Holst.)

(15) For the labourer is worthy of his hire, and sufficient for the labourer is his maintenance.

The first part of this is of course familiar to us from Luke 10, 7, but the addition of the correlative thought makes an excellent parallelism similar to others we have noticed. It comes from Epiphanius (fourth century), and it is impossible to be sure whether it is authentic or just a happy thought of his.

(16) I am he concerning whom Moses prophesied saying, A prophet shall the Lord our God raise up for you from your brethren, like unto me; hear him in all things, and whoever will not hear that prophet shall die.

This again comes from the *Clementine Homilies*. The passage quoted (Deut. 18, 15–19) occurs twice in Acts (3, 22; 7, 37) and was evidently a familiar prophecy which it was felt to have been fulfilled by Christ. That he should himself have laid hold of it and claimed it as predicting his coming seems exceedingly possible.

(17) But when the apostles asked our Lord what ought to be thought about the prophets of the Jews, who were believed formerly to have prophesied his coming, he, angry that they even now had such thoughts, answered, You have sent away the living who is before you and prate about dead men.

Augustine (354–430) speaks of this as coming from some

apocryphal scripture, but does not cite it as authoritative. It of course appears to contradict not only the previous saying here but the generally accepted view of prophecy. But it is possible to believe that while he deliberately acted in such a way as to claim to be the promised Messiah (Zech. 9, 9–Mark 11, 2, etc.), yet at the same time he might warn against stressing the past and neglecting the present. In some ways it is a very relevant and up-to-date teaching.

(18) Again the Lord said, Let him that is married not put away, and let him that is unmarried marry not; let him that with purpose of celibacy hath promised not to marry again remain unmarried.

This is from Clement of Alexandria. Is it a paraphrase of the teaching in 1 Cor. 7, 32f. or an authentic word of Jesus on which Paul based his teaching? It is not easy to feel very certain.

(19) Whoso redeemeth souls from idols, he shall be great in my kingdom.

This again is from one of the apocryphal books – the *Acts of Thomas* – where it is introduced by the words 'For thus were we taught by the Saviour who said. . . .' While the story in which it occurs is typically legendary and has no claim to authenticity, it is of course quite credible that sayings might be included which recalled words spoken by Jesus. There are no references to idols in the Gospels, but the journey made by him and his disciples to Tyre and Sidon (Mark 7, 24) would bring them within sight of idolatry at its worst and might well have been the occasion for such a word as this.

(20) The Lord Christ said to Peter, Verily thine eyes shall never be closed in eternity for the light of this world.

This is found in a book called *The Life of Schnudi*, who was an Egyptian monk in the middle of the fifth century. It incorporates much of the Two Ways document which we have noticed in a previous chapter, so the writer would seem to have been in touch with early records. But this saying is hardly likely to be more than a picturesque modification of John 8, 12 – 'I am the light of the world; he that followeth me shall not walk in darkness but have the light of life.'

(21) and (22) Two fragments of a lost *Preaching of Peter* are preserved by Clement of Alexandria as follows:

> The Lord said to the apostles, If then any of Israel will repent, to believe in God through my name, his sins shall be forgiven him. And after twelve years go ye out into the world lest any say, We did not hear.
>
> The Lord says, I chose out you twelve, judging you to be disciples worthy of me, whom the Lord willed, and thinking you faithful apostles, sending you into the world to preach the Gospel to men throughout the world, that they should know that there is one God – to declare by faith in me what shall be, that they that have heard and believed might be saved, and that they which have not believed may hear and bear witness, not having any defence so as to say, We did not hear.

The fact that it was about twelve years before the apostles dispersed from Jerusalem to preach more widely may have led to these sayings. Or may we suppose that Jesus himself did so instruct them?

CHAPTER 15

FROM GOSPEL MANUSCRIPTS

BEFORE the days of printing, when everything was written by hand, it is obvious that different copies of a book might well differ in their wording in various ways. And in the thousands of manuscripts of the New Testament – written first in Greek and then translated into Latin and Syriac and other languages – there are in fact tens of thousands of variations. By far the greater number of these are insignificant, except for highly technical studies. Letters or even words or sentences have been omitted – or duplicated. A whole line is sometimes left out – or written twice. Words and especially names have been wrongly spelt. Sometimes the mistakes were unintentional through the carelessness of scribes, sometimes they were deliberate through a desire to improve the text, as for example when the words of one Gospel are brought into harmony with those of another.

The point of interest for us in our search for extra information about Jesus is that occasionally some manuscript or manuscripts include words not found in the familiar form of the text. It is just possible that sometimes such a reading may preserve the original way in which the passage was written, the usual form being a corruption. But it is more probable that the unfamiliar words have been added by some copyist. Perhaps in the first instance he wrote something that he had heard and thought valuable in the margin of his script – from which later scribes might easily take it right into the text, thinking it was something which had been unintentionally omitted. There are many possibilities of this kind. And it is evident that such words may embody information handed down through some extraneous channel and actually preserve genuine sayings of Jesus, which we should not allow to be forgotten.

Most of these manuscripts, written on parchment or vellum and dating from the fifth century onwards, have long been the treasured possessions of monastic or other libraries, and have been studied and classified by scholars with great diligence. But during the last hundred years some more ancient copies have been discovered and also some fragmentary papyrus manuscripts – all of which has broadened considerably the basis of the textual study of the Gospel. It would take us too far from our subject to examine these discoveries fully, but one or two of the more romantic incidents may be mentioned.

It was in 1844 that Constantine Tischendorf visited the Convent of St Catherine at the foot of Mt Sinai and saw a basket in the hall full of old parchments destined for the fire; examining them he realized that they were ancient and valuable, and he was allowed to take some sheets away. He returned to the convent some years later and found the rest of the manuscript, which was eventually purchased by the Emperor of Russia and made available for scholars. It was sold to the British Museum by the Soviet government in 1933 for £100,000 – the famous Codex Sinaiticus. (A codex is a book with pages in contrast to the old roll-books.) Like the Codex Vaticanus in the Vatican Library at Rome, it dates from about 325, and these two were for a long time regarded as the oldest and best manuscripts of the New Testament; they are referred to in the margin of the Revised Version at the end of Mark's Gospel. Another important discovery at the same convent was of a very ancient Syriac version of the Gospels; in 1892, the twin sisters, Mrs Lewis and Mrs Gibson, eminent Cambridge scholars, found it and photographed it, as they were not allowed to bring it away. It is a palimpsest (which means 'twice-written') – the original Gospel script having been scratched out and a later writing of no value put on top of it, owing to paper scarcity. The task of deciphering the underlying text is of course a very tricky and highly technical one.

There have been several more recent discoveries of manuscripts. In a remote valley of the Caucasus an ancient book was kept as a sort of village fetish, but when discovered was found by scholars to be as valuable in some ways as those already mentioned; it is known as the Koridethi manuscript because it had come years before from a monastery there at the far end of the Black Sea. In 1906, a manuscript was discovered at Akhmim in Egypt and purchased in Cairo by Mr C. L. Freer of Detroit; it is now known as the Washington manuscript. It contains a long interpolation in Mark 16 which is considered later in this chapter. And most important of all, in 1931 a group of papyrus manuscripts was found in Egypt dating from about the year 200, much older that is to say than any of the great vellum copies. Sir Frederic Kenyon says 'The net result of this discovery is to reduce the gap between the earliest manuscripts and the traditional dates of the New Testament books so far that it becomes negligible in any discussion of their authenticity.'

A still more remarkable 'find' will be mentioned in the next chapter; these points are included here to help to give some suggestion of what lies behind statements about the manuscripts of the Gospels and of the hazards through which the text of the New Testament has passed in its long journey from its writers to the present day.

There is still one manuscript to be described, Codex Bezae, which is of special importance for the particular study on which we are engaged; it includes more 'extras' of one kind or another than any of the others. It is a bilingual volume (Greek and Latin) which was at Lyons in the sixteenth century and was brought from there and presented to the University of Cambridge by the reformer Theodore Beza – hence the name given to it. It is one of the greatest treasures of the University Library. Some of its readings have support from certain old Latin and Syriac manuscripts, but we cannot go into the details of such confirmatory evidence.

The best known and most interesting of these passages from this Codex is as follows:

On the same day, seeing one working on the Sabbath, he said unto him, Man, if indeed thou knowest what thou doest, blessed

art thou; but if thou knowest not, thou art cursed and a transgressor of the law.

This is found in Luke 6 in place of verse 5 ('And he said unto
them, That the Son of man is Lord also of the Sabbath'), as
part of the teaching of Jesus about Sabbath observance. He
was of course much freer in his thought about this question
than the religious leaders of his time, and this seems in full
agreement with his attitude. Many scholars have accepted
it as genuine, one stating its significance thus – 'It brings
out with marvellous force the distinction between the conscious transgression of a law recognized as binding, and the
assertion of a higher law superseding the lower.'

Another important addition in this Codex is found after
John 6, 56:

as the Father in me and I in the Father. Verily, verily, I say unto
you, unless you take the body of the Son of man as the bread of life
you have not life in him.

This does not add materially to the argument of the teaching
in that chapter, and for that very reason might easily have
been omitted accidentally.

More valuable perhaps is the addition at Matt. 10, 23
not only in 'Bezae' but in a considerable number of other
manuscripts:

and if they persecute you in the other, flee to a third.

A fairly strong case can be made out for thinking that this
is the way the text was first written and that these words
were left out for stylistic reasons – because they seemed
tautological and unnecessary. But they do really heighten
the significance of the passage in two ways – by suggesting
that persecution was likely to persist and by stressing the
need for untiring endurance.

Next we have the strange variation in the words at the
Baptism of Jesus :

this day have I begotten thee.

This is found at Luke 3, 22 in 'Bezae' and other manuscripts, and also in some early Church writers, including as we have seen the Ebionite Gospel. It is of course a quotation from Psalm 2, 7, and this psalm may have been in the thought of Jesus at this time. Canon Streeter, a great authority on the Gospels, believed that this was the correct reading in Luke, because the tendency was for scribes to bring the Gospels into harmony with each other, and it is therefore more likely that they changed this strange version to make the story the same as in Matthew and Mark than that it should have been introduced in contradiction to them.

Much the same group of manuscripts have a long interpolation at Matt. 20, 28, which is similar to the parable in Luke 14, 8–10, though the wording is quite different. Also a negative form of Matt. 18, 20 – 'For there are not two or three gathered together in my name and I not among them'. And more remarkably still the substitution in Mark 1, 41 of the word 'angered' for the familiar 'moved with compassion'. This may occasion surprise and arouse dislike, but there are strong reasons for thinking it the original form of the story. It would be very strange for compassion to be altered in the manuscripts to anger, and stranger still for Matthew and Luke (whose Gospels at this stage are based on Mark) to cut out this lovely word if it was in the copies of Mark which they used. It is just such a word as Luke especially would have loved to use – that he did not seems clear proof he did not know of it. Moreover, the anger of Jesus was surely well justified on this occasion (as on another shortly afterwards – see Mark 3, 5). The man was suffering from a contagious disease and had no right to come amongst the crowds. Of course Jesus felt compassion for him, but he sternly rebuked his thoughtlessness and ordered him to go away quickly.

Some other interesting readings in certain of the old Latin or Syriac manuscripts must be mentioned, which however are not found in 'Bezae'.

And when Jesus was being baptized, a great light shone from the water, so that all that were gathered together feared.

This occurs at Matt. 3, 17, and several ancient writers, including Justin and the Ebionite Gospel, say something of the same sort. Again in the story of the resurrection at Mark 16, 3, one manuscript has this addition:

But suddenly at the third hour of the day there came darkness throughout all the globe of the earth, and angels came down from the heavens, and rising in the glory of the living God they went up together with him, and immediately there was light. Then the women drew near to the sepulchre and saw that the stone was rolled away, for it was very great.

This is more apocryphal than most of the other manuscript additions, and indeed there is something similar to it in the 'Gospel of Peter' to which reference was made earlier. A more credible 'extra' is found in several of these manuscripts in one form or another at Luke 23, 47:

And all those which were assembled there and saw that which was done, were smiting their breasts and saying, Woe unto us, what things are done to us for our sins; for the desolation of Jerusalem hath drawn nigh.

Reference must be made to the 'Diatessaron' (which means 'through-four'), an early Harmony of the Gospels made in Syriac by Tatian, in the latter half of the second century. It is not extant in its original form, but is known in part from Latin and Arabic translations. Apparently it contained a considerable number of variations from familiar texts and also additions, in some cases agreeing with 'Bezae' and the other manuscripts already mentioned, but in others having peculiar readings of its own. One or two of these may be quoted:

Matt. 10, 29 – Are not two sparrows sold for a farthing in the tavern?
Matt. 26, 47 – And with them there was a man of the Romans.
Mark 7, 26 – the woman was a Gentile from Emesa in Syria.
John 21, 12 – But he did not appear to them in his own form.

Occasionally some other slight support is found for a reading, though probably the Diatessaron was its original location:

Matt. 17, 25 – Simon saith to him, Yea. Jesus said unto him, Then do thou also give to them as being a stranger.

Mark 7, 33 – and spitting upon his fingers, he put them in his ears.

Mark 10, 51 – The blind man said unto him, My Lord and Teacher, that thou shouldest open my eyes, and that I may see thee.

Of this addition to the Bartimaeus story, Dr Rendel Harris said, 'A more exquisite gloss, if it be a gloss, it would be difficult to imagine.' He evidently thought it might be an authentic recollection.

The next passage we shall notice is of rather doubtful value, but it is found in the manuscript commonly called the Washington Codex, to which reference has been made above. Dr Moffatt includes it in his modern translation of the New Testament, and thinks that it was an original part of the appendix to the Gospel of Mark – 16, 9–20. The lack of connexion between verses 14 and 15 has often been noted, and in this manuscript the following conversation is found:

But they excused themselves saying, This age of lawlessness and unbelief lies under the sway of Satan, who will not allow what lies under the unclean spirits to understand the truth and power of God; therefore, they said to Christ, reveal your righteousness now. Christ answered them, The limit of years for Satan's power has now expired, but other terrors are at hand. I was delivered to death on behalf of sinners that they might return to the truth and sin no more, that they might inherit that glory of righteousness which is spiritual and imperishable in heaven.

This might possibly preserve an echo of something Jesus once said, but it is more probably just the result of imaginative piety.

For the next two passages the manuscript evidence is slight but there is some good support from Church writers.

I say unto you that men must give an account in the day of judgement of every good word which they shall not speak.

This is of course a negative form of the teaching in Matt. 12, 36, and it is closely in accord with a remark of Justin

Martyr's – 'We know that everyone who can speak the truth and yet speaks it not shall be judged by God.'

Let thy holy spirit come upon us and cleanse us.

This beautiful petition was quoted by various ancient writers, including Marcion (140), as part of the Lord's Prayer in Luke 11, 2, and several modern scholars have thought it authentic. Certainly verse 13 – 'If ye then being evil know how to give good gifts to your children, how much more shall your heavenly Father give the holy spirit to them that ask him?' – seems more appropriate if this petition had preceded it. It should be remembered that in all probability Jesus taught the Prayer to his disciples on more than one occasion with variations according to particular circumstances and individuals; it was not one set of words that was important, but the true spirit and pattern of prayer.

One passage from an Armenian manuscript is of great interest:

A certain woman was taken in sins, against whom all bore witness that she was deserving of death. They brought her to Jesus to see what he would command, in order that they might malign him. Jesus made answer and said, Come ye who are without sin cast stones and stone her to death. But he himself bowing his head was writing with his finger on the earth, to declare their sins, and they were seeing their several sins on the stones. And filled with shame they departed and no one remained but only the woman. Saith Jesus, Go in peace, and present the offering for sins, as in the law is written.

This is of course an alternative form of the familiar story found at John 7, 53–8, 11, but the connexion between the two is not clear. This version does not give the definition of the woman's sin as adultery nor the words of Jesus, 'Neither do I condemn thee', and these points were felt in early days to be objectionable features of it – Augustine actually says that the story was omitted by some 'from a fear lest their wives should gain impunity in sin.' As this Armenian version eliminates these points, it may well be a modified form, intended to meet these scruples.

On the other hand, it may perhaps be right, whether through tapping a sound tradition or by a happy guess, regarding the meaning of Jesus's writing on the ground. This action has commonly caused perplexity, and it certainly lends colour to the story to think that he reminded them of their own sinfulness, not only in word but by the specification of particular sins, leaving it to their consciences to appropriate and allocate these to themselves. In which case it may not be merely a secondary version of no value.

But there is a further complication. It is generally agreed that the story was not an original part of John's Gospel; the language and style are quite different from those of that Gospel, and as the margin of the Revised Version tells us it is not found in most of the Greek manuscripts. This does not of course mean that it is not to be thought authentic – it is equally agreed that it is a genuine reminiscence of Jesus which was added to the Gospel from some good extraneous source. Now Eusebius tells us that Papias included in his book a story 'of a woman accused of many sins before the Lord', and also that the Hebrew Gospel contained it. Was either of these the 'good extraneous source'? And if one of them was, may not the other have told the story in this modified form given by the Armenian manuscript? It is impossible to be sure.

There is still another possibility. The canonical version is found in some old manuscripts after Luke 21, 38, where it fits much better into the context than it does in its usual position. Perhaps then Luke (or one of those from whom he drew information) may be the source of the story, and Papias, the Hebrew Gospel, and the Armenian manuscript may all give a secondary version which Papias or someone else modified in this way for the reasons mentioned above.

We come finally to the surprising fact that at Matt. 27, 16, 17, in quite a number of manuscripts the personal name of 'Jesus' is given to Barabbas. Origen (230) stated that he found this reading in certain very old copies – which must mean some of the second or even the first century. Now though this may not at first commend itself to us, yet the probability is that it is correct. The name Jesus (Greek form of Joshua) was a common one in those days, and the coincidence of names though strange is by no means incredible. It is hardly conceivable that such an insertion should have been made in early days, while alternatively reverence for the sacred name would readily account for its omission from many manuscripts. Many modern scholars accept it as authentic. Moffatt includes it in his translation, while Deissmann says, 'This piece of original text should be confidently restored to its place in modern revisions of the Bible.'

CHAPTER 16

FROM THE SANDS OF EGYPT

——

DURING the last hundred years, as we have already mentioned, a great deal of archaeological exploration has been carried out by both classical and Biblical scholars in the Middle East, and some remarkable discoveries have been made. Excavations amongst rubbish heaps in Egypt have yielded many fragments of papyrus, of interest and importance. A flood of light has been thrown upon language and customs in the first centuries of our era, but it is of course with the actual information about Jesus which has been unearthed that we are immediately concerned here.

In the latter part of last century Dr Flinders Petrie and others made extensive investigations in the Fayum district of Upper Egypt, and amongst other 'finds' was the famous Fayum Gospel fragment. This small piece of papyrus is now in the Archduke Rainer's collection of papyri at Vienna. It contains only a few lines with some words and letters missing, and various attempts at restoration have been made. But sufficient remains to show that it is part of the story of Jesus warning Peter about betrayal, though several words are different from those in the Gospels; 'cock' is a variant form, and 'crow' is literally 'cry cuckoo'. It is clearly not a quotation from any of the Gospels as we have them, and opinions have varied greatly about it. Was it from one of those other records of Gospel facts to which Luke referred in his introduction (Luke 1, 1–4)? Or was it a casual and incorrect quotation such as any preacher or commentator might make? In any case, as it is thought to date from the third century it is certainly one of the earliest written statements about Jesus in existence.

We come next to the sensational discovery in 1897 of a leaf of a papyrus book with seven short 'Sayings of Jesus' written on it. The discoverers were Drs Grenfell and Hunt, who were excavating on behalf of the Egypt Exploration Fund at Oxyrhynchus, an important city of ancient Egypt, situated on the edge of the desert 120 miles south of Cairo. Six years later in 1903 they made further discoveries – a piece of a papyrus roll containing other 'Sayings' and several very torn fragments of another roll apparently giving some familiar Gospel teaching but in an unfamiliar setting. The discoverers considered that all these papyri belonged to the third century, probably to the first quarter of it, the form and type of handwriting being the main determinant in this highly technical question. These discoveries created an enormous amount of interest, of course, and a large literature has gathered around them, the most varied views being held regarding their origin, authenticity, and significance. It is impossible for us to do more here than touch the fringe of these issues.

The most detailed study of these sayings was made by H. G. Evelyn White in his book *The Sayings of Jesus from Oxyrhynchus* (1920), in the course of which he argues that they are part of a literary collection of Sayings, probably drawn from the lost 'Gospel according to the Hebrews', which we have already considered. As we shall see, one of the sayings is quoted by Clement of Alexandria as from that Gospel, which is a point in favour of this theory, but there are a number of reasons against it, and there can be no certainty that all the sayings were extracted from the same source. My own view as elaborated in the *Harvard Theological Review* (January 1930) is that they were culled from various sources, canonical and uncanonical, not excluding oral tradition, and that they formed a Treasury of Sayings perhaps made for private devotional use. I am also more inclined than Evelyn White and most other scholars to believe that there is some genuine 'extra' material here, intermingled with some that is secondary and of little value. A more enthusiastic acceptance of the sayings as a whole may be quoted to show how impossible it is to be sure about these matters. Professor J. H. Moulton wrote, 'That he really uttered the sayings ascribed to him in this fragment (the first of the papyri) I cannot for a moment doubt. They are all in complete accord with his teaching, and they have just that vivid, brief, pictorial, parabolic style which no one could ever imitate, and which we must instinctively recognize as coming to us from the lips of him who spake as never man spake.'

Some of the sayings are so fragmentary and the suggested restorations so doubtful that it is best for us to ignore them here, and to concentrate attention on those that are reasonably certain and worth while.

Except ye fast toward the world ye shall not find the kingdom, and unless ye sanctify the whole week ye shall not see the Father.

I stood in the midst of the world and in the flesh was I seen of them, and I found all men drunken, and none found I athirst among them, and my soul grieveth over the sons of men, because they are blind in their heart.

Wherever there are two, they are not without God, and wherever there is one alone I say I am with him. Raise the stone and there thou shalt find me; cleave the wood and there am I.

A prophet is not acceptable in his own country, neither doth a physician work cures upon them that know him.

Let not him who seeks cease until he finds, and when he finds he shall be astonished; astonished he shall reign, and having reigned he shall rest.

His disciples say unto him, When wilt thou be manifest to us and when shall we see thee? He saith, When ye shall be stripped and not be ashamed.

The first of these sayings is a strong plea for sincerity and sacrifice as essential for true spiritual experience. The third emphasizes the thought of honest toil as the way to realize the presence of God. The fifth is quoted by Clement as from the Hebrew Gospel, and seems to be an elaboration of the call to seek first God's kingdom (Matt. 6, 33) and so to be members of his sovereign people. The last perhaps means that to bear indignity and persecution, despising the shame (Mark 8, 38), is to receive heavenly vision, as in the case of Stephen (Acts 7, 56). Together they seem to stress in a valuable manner the thoughts of the challenge and the blessing of the Gospel message.

In 1908, Grenfell and Hunt discovered a single vellum leaf containing a longer passage than those already considered, and in my view one of considerable value. They thought that the writing belonged to the fourth century, but that the unknown Gospel of which it preserves an extract was probably composed in the second. The opening and closing sentences of the leaf are mutilated, and we need not linger over them. The main passage is as follows:

And he took them and brought them into the very place of purification, and was walking with them in the temple. And a certain Pharisee, a high priest whose name was Levi, met them and said to the Saviour, Who gave thee leave to walk in this place of purification and to see these holy vessels, when thou hast not washed nor yet have thy disciples bathed their feet? But defiled thou hast walked in this temple, which is a pure place, wherein no other man walks except he has washed himself and changed his garments, neither does he venture to see these holy vessels. And the Saviour straightway stood still with his disciples and answered him, Art thou then being here in the temple clean? He saith unto him, I am clean, for I washed in the pool of David, and having descended by one staircase I ascended by another and put on white and clean garments, and then I came and looked upon these holy vessels. The Saviour answered and said unto him, Woe ye blind, who see not! Thou hast washed in these running waters wherein dogs and swine have been cast night and day, and thou hast cleansed and wiped the outside skin which also harlots and flute-girls anoint and wash and wipe and beautify for the lust of men, but within they are full of scorpions and all wickedness. But I and my disciples who thou sayest have not bathed have been dipped in the waters of eternal life which come from God.

The general view of this story has been that it is unauthentic and inaccurate about details of topography and temple ritual. But Buchler in the *Jewish Quarterly Review* put up a strong argument that 'tradition fully confirms the details which sound so incredible.' Dr Swete also argued that the style of the fragment is similar to that of the Synoptics and quite unlike later apocryphal books, and he thought that the lost Gospel from which it came 'may be supposed to embody traditions which were current in Egypt during the quarter of a century which followed the close of the Apostolic age.' For these and other reasons I believe that we have here an account of a real incident, elaborated and embellished at some points though it may be.

The reference to the defilement of the water in which the priest had bathed is very apt and brings us to the heart of the story. It was running water, and however pure it might look it had on its long journey to the temple received many defilements, and the reminder of this is a subtle way of suggesting the uselessness of skin-deep purification. The biting irony of the reference to the care bestowed upon the skin by harlots is reminiscent of, though entirely distinct from, Christ's condemnation of the scribes and Pharisees in Matt. 23, while the woe upon their spiritual blindness is paralleled in verses 16 and 24 of that chapter.

The last of the fragments unearthed by Grenfell and Hunt was published in 1914. It is unfortunately very mutilated; in fact only a few lines at the top of four columns (two on each side of the leaf) remain. It is thought to belong to the fourth century and to be part of an uncanonical Gospel, the date of the composition of which may of course be much earlier. It apparently purports to be a personal narrative in which Jesus and some unnamed disciple figure, and it has been thought an extract from the apocryphal Gospel of Peter to which reference has been made earlier; there are however several difficulties about this. Some of the restorations of defective words are admittedly conjectural, but on the basis of them the following translation is given:

overcame me. And Jesus stood by in a vision and said, Why art thou cast down? For it is not thou who . . . but he who gave . . .

thou didst say . . . making no answer. What then hast thou forbidden? What is the new doctrine that they say thou teachest or what the new baptism that thou dost preach?

The scribes and Pharisees and priests seeing him had indignation because he reclined in the midst of sinners. And Jesus hearing them said, They that are whole need not a physician.

. . . Pray for your enemies. For he that is not against you is with you, and he that today is afar off shall tomorrow be near you . . . adversary.

I have very tentatively suggested an alternative arrangement, the last two fragments being read before the first two – in other words the leaf being reversed. In that case it is just possible that we have here part of the story of James, not Peter – beginning with a brief summary of what he heard and saw in the Galilean days when he was in antagonism to Jesus (Mark 3, 21, 31), and followed by an account of the resurrection appearance to which Paul (1 Cor. 15, 7) and the Hebrew Gospel (as we have seen) refer, and part of the conversation that resulted. This is quite speculative, of course, and no reliance is to be placed upon it, but it seems as good as any other guess, and there the matter must rest until more data are discovered. It is all rather tantalizing!

Two other important discoveries of papyrus must now be referred to. The first is a tiny scrap of the Fourth Gospel in the possession of the John Rylands Library at Manchester, which is dated with some confidence to the first half of the second century A.D. On one side of it are parts of verses 31–3 of Chapter 18, and on the other parts of verses 37–8 of the same chapter. Its importance is out of all proportion to its size, for it is almost certainly the earliest known fragment of any part of the New Testament. Moreover it is probably the earliest witness to the existence of this Gospel and proves that it must have been written considerably earlier than scholars have often supposed.

The other discovery is of four small fragments in the possession of the British Museum; they were published by H. Idris Bell and T. C. Skeat in 1935, and a valuable study of them appeared in the *Bulletin of the John Rylands Library* by Dr Dodd the following year, under the title 'A New Gospel'. The papyrus is believed to date from about the middle of the second century and the unknown Gospel of which it is a copy is thought to belong to the very early part of that century, perhaps even to the end of the first. It contains the same kind of material that we have in the canonical Gospels, and shows various links with them, especially with John, but it is not a part of any of them or of the known apocryphal Gospels. The restorations of missing or mutilated words and letters are regarded as fairly certain, and on the basis of them the following translation is given:

Turning to the rulers of the people he spoke this saying, Search the scriptures – those in which you suppose that you have life are the ones which bear witness concerning me. Do not think that I have come to accuse you to my Father – your accuser is Moses on whom you have set your hope. And when they said, We know well that God spake to Moses, but we do not know whence you come, Jesus said in reply, Now your belief is accused. . . .

. . . that they should drag him . . . and taking up stones together should stone him. And the rulers laid hands upon him to seize him and hand him over to the crowd, and they could not seize him, because the hour of his arrest had not yet come. But Jesus himself going out from their hands departed from them.

And behold, a leper approached him and said, Rabbi Jesus, when I was travelling with lepers and eating with them at the inn, I became leprous myself also. If therefore you will, I shall be cleansed. Then the Lord said, I will, be clean. And at once the leprosy departed from him. And the Lord said to him, Go and show yourself to the priests.

. . . came to him and tested him by examination saying, Rabbi Jesus, we know that you have come from God, for the things you are doing bear witness beyond all the prophets. Tell us then is it lawful to pay to kings those things which pertain to the government? Shall we pay or shall we not? And Jesus knowing their mind indignantly said to them, Why do you call me Rabbi, when you do not listen to what I say? Finely did Isaiah prophesy concerning you saying, This people honour me with their lips, but their heart is far from me. In vain do they worship me . . . commandments. . . .

Jesus as he walked stood still upon the verge of the river Jordan, and stretching out his right hand he filled it with water and sprinkled it upon the shore. And thereupon the water made the ground moist, and it was watered before them and brought forth fruit.

Much of this is familiar to us from the Gospels, but some sentences are linked together differently from what we are accustomed to. The double form of address 'Rabbi Jesus' which occurs twice is not found in the Gospels and probably means that the document is less primitive than they are. The significance of the closing scene is not clear – it may have told a legendary nature miracle of which we have no other account, or it may have been a symbolic parabolic action. On the whole, we cannot place much credence upon the historicity of these narratives, but they are certainly much superior to the apocryphal Gospels and they show a remarkable familiarity with Gospel facts and disputations which evidently existed in Egypt within about a hundred years of the crucifixion.

One further point may be mentioned. All the above papyri are written in Greek, which of course was the *lingua franca* in Egypt as elsewhere in those days. But there are also some Coptic or Old Egyptian papyri on which words of Jesus are found, similar to those in the Gospels but varying from them somewhat as those we have just been studying. These can be found in Dr M. R. James's *Apocryphal New Testament*, to which reference has already been made. They apparently date from the fourth and fifth centuries, but of course may be based on much earlier material.

CHAPTER 17

SOME PROBLEM PASSAGES

———

THERE are some interesting passages which do not fall into any of the categories already dealt with but which I hesitate to put amongst the definitely spurious (see Chapter 19). They are of late date, but that does not necessarily rule them out as of no value. Most of them are from Moslem books and we will devote our next chapter to them. But first there are a few from Christian writings which we will examine here.

We notice first those found in an Arabic treatise discovered by Mrs M. D. Gibson (see above, p. 122) in the Convent of St Catherine at Mt Sinai and entitled by her 'On the Triune Nature of God'. The manuscript belongs to the eighth or ninth century, and the work cannot be much earlier as it is a polemic against the Moslems. Mrs Gibson argued that this is not conclusive against the antiquity of its Biblical text, and Rendel Harris agreed – 'It is quite within the bounds of possibility that the Gospels known to our writer had independent readings, and perhaps some pre-canonical elements.' Five passages from it may be mentioned.

(1) In the story of the healing of the palsy, the priests are present, and Jesus addresses his argument to them, 'O company of priests, whether is it easier for me to say. . . .' It is interesting that in the Moslem agrapha, to which we refer in the next chapter, he is often represented as saying, 'O company of the disciples . . .'

(2) In the story of the man with the withered hand, his question to the onlookers regarding doing good or evil on the Sabbath is answered thus, 'Nay, let us do good on the Sabbath and let life be saved.' He then replies, 'Ye speak truly.' This of course contradicts the canonical statement that they were silent.

(3) There is an odd statement that the apostles said to Jesus,

'Thy speech is the speech of light to those who go and call upon thee.'

(4) In the narrative of the Entry, there are a number of points of contact with the version in the *Dialogue of Timothy and Aquila* which, as we saw in a previous chapter, probably preserves some primitive material. Both, for example, state that olive branches were pulled down from the trees and used in the demonstration of welcome.

(5) The account of the Ascension contains this teaching: 'I send you this day as sheep among wolves, but tarry ye in the holy house until ye are clothed with power from heaven. I go to where I was, and I will send you the Paraclete, the Holy Spirit, the Righteous One, whom men cannot look upon, him who will bring me to your remembrance and everything of which I have spoken to you. He will speak in your mouths, and ye shall be led before kings of the earth and rulers. Be not at all troubled about what ye shall speak, for the Spirit whom I shall send unto you, he shall speak in your mouths.'

None of these passages carries very strong conviction; though, if the writer was indeed in touch with the second-century document in the background of the *Dialogue of Timothy and Aquila*, they deserve respect. As regards the last, it has often seemed strange that so much of the teaching in preparation for persecution comes so early in the Gospel (Matt. 10).

The next passage and those in the following paragraph were strangely enough discovered in Britain. It occurs in Latin as the text of an Old English sermon of the twelfth century:

Be ye brave in war, and fight with the old serpent, and ye shall receive an everlasting kingdom.

There is no suggestion that the writer thought this of less authenticity than the other texts he used in his 'Homilies', and the opening words of the sermon certainly sound as though he had drawn it from some Gospel narrative which he accepted as genuine and valued highly:

This word which I now declare unto thee, our Lord uttered at a time when he dwelt in the land of Jerusalem, and admonished all that were there to fight bravely; and because the fight was strong to master and difficult to undertake, he promised them great reward, provided they would undertake the conflict.

Neither the metaphor, 'the old serpent', nor the illustration of the Christian life as a fight is found in the Gospels, but they are both familiar from other passages in the New Testament (Rev. 12, 9; 1 Tim. 6, 12), and it would be agreeable to think that Jesus himself spoke in some such way as this. But it must be regarded as very doubtful. This however may be said, that the occurrence of this passage and of those we shall next examine, seems to show that some unidentified apocryphal Gospel or expository book (like that of Papias) was current in England at the time these homilies were written – and that it apparently had reference to the ministry of Jesus rather than to the more usual topics of apocryphal romance, the nativity and childhood of Jesus, or events after the resurrection. Dr Richard Morris, who edited these homilies, thought this was so, calling attention to references in this sermon to the Twelve and to someone else named 'N' (Nathanael or Nicodemus?) for whose saint-day it was prepared. There are two slightly variant versions of the sermon, one in the library of Lambeth Palace, and the other in that of Trinity College, Cambridge.

We examine next some passages found in the *Blickling Homilies*, the manuscript of which, in the library of Blickling Hall, Norfolk, was transcribed and translated by Dr Morris for the Early English Text Society. A statement in the manuscript gives 971 as the date when it was penned, but Dr Morris judges from the style and vocabulary that the sermons were written in the previous century, roughly in the time of King Alfred. Unlike the sermon just considered, these were written in Anglo-Saxon and are probably older than our earliest copies of the Anglo-Saxon Gospels. They contain a good deal that may be just loose quotation or paraphrase, as for example the following:

Martha, Martha, be thou heedful and mindful of the things of Mary, that is, that thou at all times perform the will of God, which is the one best thing wherewith thou mayest please God. Mary hath chosen the best part, which shall never be taken from her.

But there are also a number of statements that look as though they might be based on extra information. For instance, Peter is named as the disciple who asked permission to go and bury his father, and Peter and John are named as the two who were sent to fetch the ass upon which Jesus sat. Of Judas it is said that 'the apostles allowed him to carry their wallets, because they wished thereby to try his covetousness.'

But the most interesting passages are the following which definitely seem to suggest uncanonical teaching, though of course the point remains to be considered whether or not it can be deemed authentic:

(1) Let us be mindful of what Christ has commanded us in the Gospel. He has said that we should, every twelve-month, give (to God) the tithe of our increase.

(2) It is written in Christ's books that the Lord himself said that the tenth part of our goods were under our own control, both as regards land and other possessions and other acquisitions.

(3) Christ himself said that he will not hear the negligent and forgetful man's prayers.

(4) We know that Christ himself said by his own mouth, When ye see growing and blowing all the fruits of the earth, and the fragrant odours exhaling from plants, then soon afterwards they shall dry up and dwindle away on account of the summer's heat.

(5) Christ himself said, Ye have me ever present among believing men, through the glory of my divine nature.

(6) Concerning those (evil) judges, Christ himself hath spoken, saying, Judge now, as ye will that ye be judged hereafter at the last day of this world.

(7) Ye need not be sad or troubled in your hearts, for I will intercede for you with the Father, that he may preserve you through his heavenly power.

(8) I will not leave you without a leader, but I will send you the Paraclete.

There is no precept in the Gospels regarding tithing (see passages 1 and 2 here) but it certainly became a practice of the Church and some such teaching of Jesus is far from unlikely – that it is a right thing to do but that it must be a voluntary not a compulsory act. The variant forms of familiar teaching in the last two passages are interesting, in particular the word 'leader' which reminds us that 'Paraclete' means much more than 'Comforter', as it is rendered in the Authorized Version of the Gospel.

Are all these the results of imaginative comment on the Gospels or does some unknown documentary source lie behind them? In favour of the latter possibility is the definiteness of the recurrent phrase 'Christ himself' – elaborated in one instance by the words 'by his own mouth'. Very little notice has been taken of these sayings, the only real study of them so far as I know being my own article in the *Expositor* in April 1925. One scholar, A. T. Cadoux, referred to passage 4 in his book *The Parables of Jesus*, and thought it preserved a memory of genuine teaching.

We come now to the last of these problem passages, the lovely little story of Jesus healing a wounded animal. There is, unfortunately, considerable mystery surrounding it. It was included some years ago by a German writer, Julius Boehmer, in a collection of Early Christian parallels to the New Testament. He drew it from an earlier writer, but failed to trace its history owing to the latter's death. The only account of it he could find was a statement that it had been found in a Coptic Bible manuscript in the Paris Library. Search there however proved unsuccessful, and there the matter rests. It is usually considered to be an extract from some Coptic apocryphal work, of which there are many in existence.

It happened that the Lord went forth from the city and walked with his disciples over the mountains. And they came to a mountain, and the road which led to it was steep. There they found a man with a sumpter-mule. But the animal had fallen for the burden was too heavy, and he beat it that it bled. And Jesus came to him and said, Man, why dost thou beat thine animal? Seest thou not that it is too weak for its burden, and knowest thou not that it suffers pains? But the man answered and said, What is that to you? I can beat it as much as I please, since it is my property, and I bought it for a good sum of money. Ask those that are with thee, for they know me and know thereof. And some of the disciples said, Yea Lord, it is as he says. We have seen how he bought it. But the Lord said, Do you not notice how it bleeds, and hear you not how it laments and cries? But they answered and said, Nay Lord, we hear not how it laments and cries. And the Lord was sad and exclaimed, Woe to you, that ye hear not how it complains to the Creator in heaven, and cries for mercy. But three times woe to him of whom it complains and cries in its distress. And he came forth and touched the animal. And it arose and its wounds were healed. And Jesus said to the man, Now go on and beat it no more, that you also may find mercy.

One would like to feel that this actually happened. It is entirely in the spirit of the Gospels – we may recall the teaching about a sparrow falling to the ground (Matt. 10, 29). But kindness to animals was an aspect of Christian charity which the Early Church largely ignored; and this fact would explain such an incident as this falling out of notice. Moreover, the restraint with which the story is told and the absence of legendary accretions is remarkable; it would have been in line with the usual tendency of apocryphal writings if most marvellous things had been described – the mule taking part in the conversation, and so forth. Reasons like these certainly arouse some queries in the mind whether an actual incident may not lie in the background here. But of course it must remain a great Perhaps.

CHAPTER 18
EVIDENCE FROM ISLAM

It may at first come as a surprise to many that we should include in our study any reference at all to Islam, for Mohammed was not born till more than 500 years after Christ. But the fact is that there are quite a number of passages in Moslem writings which at least demand attention in this connexion. We may decide that they are of no value at all, but there certainly seems a possibility to the contrary.

In the Koran itself there are about twenty passages where Jesus is mentioned, usually as 'son of Mary' and often as 'the Messiah'. There are many clear links both with the canonical and with the apocryphal Gospels, but definite teaching against the divinity of Christ. He is spoken of as 'only God's apostle and his Word which he cast into Mary and a spirit from him', and God is represented as having 'brought him the Gospel and put gentleness and compassion in the hearts of those who followed him.' The most striking passage is as follows:

And I come to confirm the law which was revealed before me, and to allow unto you as lawful part of that which hath been forbidden you; and I come unto you with a sign from your Lord; therefore fear God and obey me. Verily God is my Lord and your Lord; therefore serve him. This is the right way. But when Jesus perceived their unbelief, he said, Who will be my helpers towards God? The apostles answered, We will be helpers of God.

The opening sentence here reminds us of Matt. 5, 17, with its practical outcome as regards the Sabbath (Mark 3, 4), and the question of food (Mark 7, 15); 'my Lord and your Lord' is not far removed from John 20, 17; and 'fear God and obey me' crystallizes the teaching of many passages and is in itself a fine precept.

But the much more important question with which we have to deal is that of the sayings attributed to Jesus in the *Hadith* or traditional literature of Islam, especially in books by ascetic writers. The first notice of these that I have traced in Christian writers is that of Levinus Warnerus (1644); one of the four that he quoted is as follows:

Whoso craves wealth is like a man who drinks sea-water; the more he drinks, the more he increases his thirst, and he ceases not to drink until he perishes.

Other writers quoted this and a few more sayings in the course of their studies of various subjects; for example, Farrar in his *Life of Christ* referred to this as 'striking'. One of the most beautiful stories told of Jesus in this literature is that of the dead dog, thus:

He one day walked with his apostles and they passed by the carcase of a dog. The apostles said, How foul is the smell of this dog! But Jesus said, How white are its teeth!

The old Persian poet Nizami, in the twelfth century, wrote a poem upon this, though it was current centuries before his date. Several English verses have been written upon it.

But probably the most famous of these Moslem agrapha is that discovered by Alexander Duff, the Scottish missionary, in 1849 on the gateway of the mosque at Fatehpur-Sikri near Agra, built by Akbar, the great Mogul emperor:

The world is merely a bridge; ye are to pass over it and not build your dwellings upon it.

Duff's description of this and comment upon it in his *Life* (1879) are interesting, and Miss C. F. Gordon-Cumming, in her travel volume *In the Himalayas* (1884), also describes it. It is one of the only two agrapha included under that heading in the *Encyclopaedia Britannica*, which suggests the measure of neglect this whole study has suffered. A useful devotional comment on it was made by David Smith in his *Unwritten Sayings of our Lord*; he mentioned the fact that there were no bridges in Palestine in the time of Christ and that the word does not occur in the Bible. He suggested that nevertheless the saying might be genuine and date from the journey made by Jesus and his disciples to Phoenicia (Mark 7, 24), which would bring them within sight of the famous mole at Tyre – along which they may even have walked.

We come now to the two largest collections of this material. In 1893–4, Professor D. S. Margoliouth, of Oxford University, contributed a series of articles to the *Expository Times* in which he gathered seventy-seven such passages, chiefly culled from a work called *The Revival of the Religious Sciences* by Al Ghazzali, one of the finest of the mystical writers of Islam, who lived in the eleventh century but drew upon much older sources. Then in 1916 and 1927, a still longer collection was published by Professor Asin of Madrid University. It consists of 233 passages, which include practically all of Margoliouth's collection, with others from Al Ghazzali and from many other writers in addition.

Some of these passages contain legendary and even magical tales of the type familiar to us from the apocryphal Gospels, some deal with Mary and John the Baptist and other characters rather than with Jesus, some are evidently loose quotations or paraphrases of the Gospels, some show clear signs of having been framed for doctrinal reasons in opposition to the thought of Christ's divinity. But a considerable number remain which seem to be quite independent of the Gospels and to bear comparison with some of the more familiar agrapha from other sources. The question for us to consider is whether it is possible that they contain any authentic reminiscence at all of Jesus or whether they are entirely fictional.

There is no doubt about the extraordinary fertility of invention amongst early Moslem writers – their books contain many traditions regarding their prophet, of which only a small percentage can be deemed genuine. It is not surprising then that they allowed their imaginations to play around the figure of Jesus whom they evidently much admired, and it is probable that this is sufficient explanation of most of the agrapha we are considering. The point to be resolved is whether there is any reason to suppose that a little good grain may somehow have survived amongst the mass of chaff. Margoliouth and most other writers who have commented upon them do not appear to think so, but there is certainly something to be said on the other side.

Asin called attention to the absence of dogmatic purpose in most of these sayings, and thought that the motive behind them evidently was the desire to give the authority of Jesus to certain moral and ascetic teachings. He considered that, in view of the known influx of Arabian Christians (Nestorians and others) into Islam, the presence of some traditional elements cannot be deemed impossible. He made much of the argument that in the arid soil of Islam there was produced the plant of monasticism, and that no other explanation is possible than that it grew from a Christian seed. While he disclaimed any attempt to assign each of these agrapha to its correct source or to assess their value finally, he was clearly of opinion that authentic matter is involved and that they are of greater worth than has commonly been supposed.

My own contribution to this subject appeared in the *Expository Times* in 1928 (January and February). In the course of it I developed the point made by Asin that the eastward movement of the Church almost certainly influenced Islam more than has often been thought, and that this may well have involved the handing on of some otherwise unrecorded sayings of Jesus. That Rome was in those days the strategic centre of the world is more evident to us than it can have been to the Early Church, and those who had received the commission to preach the Gospel to all nations would naturally go east and south as well as north and west. The evidence that they did so is interestingly advanced in Professor John Foster's little book *Beginning from Jerusalem* (1955). It is perfectly possible then that in some out-of-the-way corners of Arabia and Mesopotamia some good traditions and ancient writings may for long have been cherished. Dr Bigg believed that the *Clementine Homilies*, in which, as we have seen, several agrapha are found, originated in one 'of those Jewish communities which refused to cast in their lot with the Catholic Church. They maintained themselves in some sort of vitality down to Moslem times, and traces of their influence can be discovered in Islam.' He speaks of a Moslem writer of the tenth century giving a glimpse of such a remote little company 'dwelling in the fens between the Arabian desert, the Euphrates, and the Tigris'.

Now while it is not of course possible to enter fully into the question of the authenticity of many particular sayings, there are a few points that may usefully be made.

(1) Where any information is available about the source of a passage we should surely enquire whether the ascription to Jesus is definite, unchallenged, and of early date. If it is, and especially if several witnesses agree about it, it at least deserves our respect. Take for example the following:

> God revealed to Jesus, When I come to the heart of one of my servants and find therein nothing of love either for this world or for the future life, then with love of me will I fill him and hold him in my care as a friend.

Asin quotes several writers other than Al Ghazzali as agreeing on the authority from whom this comes, in one case a link being affirmed with Damascus – one of the most likely places from which good traditions might come. Remembering that the Gospels contain examples of what may be termed the spiritual autobiography of Jesus (the temptation story, for instance), this seems just the kind of thing he might tell his friends on one of those holy occasions when he spoke to them of his inner life. The hymn attributed to Francis Xavier –

> My God, I love Thee, – not because
> I hope for heaven thereby,

might almost have been written in exposition of it.

(2) Again, if a passage includes teaching which is alien

to or actually opposed to Islam, this should clearly raise a query as to its possible Christian origin. It is of course not always certain what does contradict Islam, for the Koran and its commentators are not entirely consistent. But some points do seem fairly definite, especially in regard to the asceticism which is so prominent in many of these sayings. Here Dr Rendel Harris may be quoted; he says that the Moslem writers 'reinforced their ascetic teaching, for which there is little enough in the way of encouragement in the Koran, by an appeal to the authority and teaching of Jesus. This they could not have done if Jesus had not appeared for them in the light of an ascetic or at least a mystical teacher. That sets one thinking at once. . . . Our own current interpretation of Jesus has always minimized the ascetic element in his teaching and has made little of its mystical side. . . . Quite other appears to have been the view of the Sufi saints and confessors.' To this may be added his comment on this striking passage:

Have no regard to the riches of the Gentiles, who are of this world, for the dazzle of their riches will take away the light of your faith.

'What makes me think this saying is genuine,' Dr Harris says, 'is not merely its evident spiritual value, but the fact that it is expressed in Biblical language. What has a Moslem to do with "riches of the Gentiles"? But in Isaiah it says, "Ye shall eat the riches of the Gentiles", and Jesus appears to be contradicting the prophecy and setting it on one side. It must be true.'

A few other passages with this ascetic and unworldly tone may be quoted:

I indeed love poverty – riches I hold in hatred.

Lay up your treasure with him who will not waste it, for loss may be feared by him who possesses the treasure of this world, but not by him who possesses the treasure of God.

Splendour in dress, pride in the heart.

Jesus said, There are three harmful things about wealth. A man may acquire it from an unlawful source. They asked, But if he acquire it from a lawful source? He replied, He may spend it on things which are objectionable. They said, But what if he spend it on legitimate things? He replied, The care of it may hinder him from the remembrance of God.

Of all ways of addressing him, the most pleasing to him was when one said, O poor man!

Of this Dr Harris says 'This is pretty strong – I will not say stronger than the Gospels. St Francis would arise and denounce me if I did. We may have undervalued the Christian tradition as to the poor man to whom the kingdom of Heaven belongs.' He proceeds to make an interesting suggestion about the primitive Jewish-Christian sect of the Ebionites, who were mistakenly thought by some early Fathers to be followers of a certain Ebion, which is literally 'poor man'. Dr Harris thinks that this tradition means that, notwithstanding less admirable characteristics, they preserved the memory of the poverty of Jesus, his love of the simple life, and his preference for a lowly manner of address.

(3) In a number of these sayings there is an aptness and conciseness of expression which reminds us forcibly of the precision and pointedness so noticeable in many Gospel texts – there is just that fitness which marks so many canonical sayings of Jesus. They put aspects of truth so well that, once known, they almost inevitably enter into our religious vocabulary. Several of those already quoted illustrate this point – here are a few other examples:

Take not the world for your lord, lest it take you for its slaves.

He who sows malice shall reap repentance.

Revere God in the secrecy of your hearts as you revere him in public.

He who asks pardon from God for those who have done him injury puts an evil spirit to flight.

As Jesus passed by the seaside, he saw some fullers at work and said to them, Ye cleanse these clothes but cleanse not your hearts.

Be in the midst, yet walk on one side.

The last of these seems to me a striking statement of the familiar teaching and prayer of Jesus that his disciples are to be in the world but not of the world (John 17, 9–18).

(4) Finally, it is worth underlining the fact that various scholars have treated this material with respect and not just ruled it all out as spurious. I have already mentioned Dr Rendel Harris's high opinion of several sayings and also the use made of one or two by Dr Farrar and Dr David Smith. Professor Guillaume, in his learned work *The Traditions of Islam*, quoted Asin's view of these sayings with approval. Dr Mingana, of Woodbrooke College, Birmingham, published a few passages which he had found in a rare Arabic work of the thirteenth century entitled *The Book of the Beautiful Admonition*. Two of them may be quoted:

Leave the world and meditate over death. To a believer death comes with good which has no evil after it, but to a wicked man it comes with an evil which has no good after it.

O doctors and teachers of the Law! You have sat down in the way to the world to come; you do not walk in it yourselves in order to reach heaven, and you do not permit others to walk in it and to reach heaven. But the ignorant is more excusable than the learned.

Mingana remarks about the sayings generally, 'To say that they have simply been invented by the writers who quoted them is an hypothesis which does not seem to be very attractive.' Again, Dr A. T. Cadoux, in his book *The Parables of Jesus*, quotes the 'sea-water' saying with approval, and also the following little tale which he says 'has every internal mark of genuineness':

Jesus said to the apostles, How would you do if you saw your brother sleeping, and the wind had lifted up his garment? They said, We would cover him up. He said, Nay, ye would uncover him! They said, God forbid! Who would do this? He said, One of you who hears a word concerning his brother, and adds to it, and relates it with additions.

It is certainly an interesting and telling little story – none of us thinks that he gossips! The illustration is very clever –

'sleeping' suggests the ignorance of the man regarding what people are saying; the wind typifies the uncertain and often quite innocent origin of these unhappy murmurs; while the deliberate uncovering aptly represents the careless and unkindly development of the tale. It might well enshrine an actual reminiscence.

Now of course none of these points amounts to demonstration, and we may not feel complete confidence about accepting any particular sayings as genuine. But it certainly seems unsatisfactory to rule them all out as imaginative exaggeration, and personally I take the view that genuine fragments are included even though we cannot reach any high degree of certainty about the identification of them.

As most of this material is not easily available to general readers it may be mentioned that some years ago a comprehensive collection of these passages was published (1929) under the title *Christ in Islam* by James Robson, Professor of Arabic in Manchester University. It has a brief introduction in which there is much the same assessment of them as I have given here.

One final point. There is a strange medieval Moslem romance entitled *The Gospel of Barnabas*, extant only in one Italian manuscript which was translated into English and published in 1907 by L. & L. Ragg. It retells the Gospel story in the interests of Islam, Jesus being made to predict the coming of Mohammed, and so forth. It seems to be the work of some renegade Christian, and its only point of interest for us is that there seems to be a slight chance that he made use of an early apocryphal book of the same name as he gave to his own work; it is known that there was an apocryphal Gospel attributed to Barnabas in the fifth century. The editors are inclined to accept the possibility and mention a few parables 'of great beauty' which they think may perhaps have derived from it. One of them is as follows:

There was a man who had great possessions, and in his territory he had desert land that only bore unfruitful things. And so, as he was walking one day through such desert land he found among such unfruitful plants a plant that had delicate fruits. Whereupon he said, Now how doth this plant here bear these so delicate fruits? Assuredly I will not that it be cut down and put on the fire with the rest. And having called his servants, he made them dig it up and set it in his garden. Even so I tell you that our God shall reserve from the flames of hell those who work righteousness, wheresoever they be.

This is quite opposed to the teaching of Islam that followers of other religions would perish – it reminds us much more of Acts 10, 35 – 'in every nation he that feareth him and worketh righteousness is accepted with him.' But the chance of it coming from Jesus himself is remote.

CHAPTER 19

SPURIOUS EVIDENCE

REFERENCE was made in an earlier chapter to the vast quantities of apocryphal books of all kinds produced in ancient times, almost all of which lie outside the scope of this work. There are however one or two points that must be mentioned, because some readers may quite possibly look for them here and not understand the omission of them.

There is, first, the story of King Abgar of Edessa writing to Jesus and receiving a reply from him. Eusebius, the historian of the early Church, states that he extracted these letters from the archives of Edessa and translated them from Syriac word for word. There is no reason to doubt this statement, but of course the age and the authority of the documents are quite a different matter. The letters are as follows:

A copy of a letter written by Abgarus the toparch to Jesus and sent by him by means of Ananias the runner, to Jerusalem:

Abgarus Uchama the toparch to Jesus the good Saviour that hath appeared in the parts of Jerusalem, greeting. I have heard concerning thee and thy cures, that they are done of thee without drugs or herbs; for as the report goes, thou makest blind men to see again, lame to walk, and cleanest lepers, and castest out unclean spirits and devils, and those that are afflicted with long sickness thou healest, and raisest the dead. And having heard all this of thee, I had determined one of two things, either that thou art God come down from heaven, and so doest these things, or art a Son of God that doest these things. Therefore now have I written and entreated thee to trouble thyself to come to me and heal the affliction which I have. For indeed I have heard that the Jews even murmur against thee and wish to do thee hurt. And I have a very little city but comely which is sufficient for us both.

The answer, written by Jesus, sent by Ananias the runner to Abgarus the toparch:

Blessed art thou that hast believed in me, not having seen me. For it is written concerning me that they that have seen me shall not believe in me, and that they that have not seen me shall believe and live. But concerning that which thou hast written to me to come unto thee – it must needs be that I fulfil all things for the which I was sent here, and after fulfilling them should then be taken up unto him that sent me. And when I am taken up, I will send thee one of my disciples to heal thine affliction and give life to thee and them that are with thee.

Copies of these letters have been found on Greek papyri dating from the fourth or fifth century, and also on a lintel discovered at Ephesus. These contain a closing sentence with the promise – 'and thy town shall be blessed and no enemy again shall have dominion over it for ever.' If this sentence was in the copy known to Eusebius he may have omitted it because it was contradicted by historical events, the city having been sacked by the Romans in 116.

The story is found in full in the apocryphal *Doctrine of Addai*. It tells how after the ascension the apostle Judas Thomas sent Addai (or some versions say Thaddeus), one of the Seventy to Abgar, who is healed and converted with large numbers of his people. Contrary to the usual run of apocryphal tales, Addai is not depicted as dying a martyr, though his successor Aggai is. And here a remarkable point emerges; Aggai was killed so suddenly that he had no time to ordain his successor Palut, who was therefore obliged to go to Antioch for ordination by Serapion there. Now Serapion became Bishop in 190, and cannot possibly have ordained one whose predecessor once removed was one of the Seventy. This anachronism betrays the legendary character of the story, and makes it probable that Christianity reached Edessa somewhere about the middle of the second century. The date of the first Christian Abgar is 200, and it is remarkable that there should be a Christian king there at such an early date.

There is another point of interest in the *Doctrine of Addai*. Before leaving Jerusalem to return to Edessa, Abgar's messenger is said to have painted a likeness of Jesus 'in choice colours', which Abgar when he received it put in a place of honour. Later on, many legends and superstitions grew up around this idea – that it was miraculously painted without human hands, and also that it was impressed on a linen cloth by Jesus himself. Copies of it and of the letters were constantly used as charms during the Middle Ages both in Britain and on the Continent. Similarly, Luke is said to have been a painter and to have been given divine help to produce a portrait of Jesus. The woman with an issue of blood is stated by Eusebius to have been a native of Caesarea Philippi, and he says that he had seen her house there and a statue of her and Jesus healing her. Later legends told of her meeting Jesus on the way to the cross and wiping his face with a towel which retained the blood-stained image upon it. Her name is given as Bernice, which was rendered into Latin as Veronica – later on wrongly explained as meaning 'vera icon', true image.

None of these tales are strictly traditional, that is, going back to early days, and none of them has any claims to be thought historical. This is true also of the so-called 'Letter of Lentulus' with its description of the physical appearance of Jesus, of which there is no trace before the thirteenth century; and of the alleged discovery of the cross by Helena, the mother of the Emperor Constantine – supposed frag-ments of which were long cherished as sacred relics. The beautiful legend of 'Quo Vadis', though possibly preserving the memory of a spiritual experience of Peter, has nothing to give us regarding the historic Jesus, and has no place in our study.

We come now to the question of Joseph of Arimathea and even Jesus himself visiting Britain. This fanciful tale may be summarized thus: Joseph is said to have been the uncle of the Virgin Mary, and to have gained his wealth by import-ing tin from Cornwall to the east. On one of his visits he brought Jesus with him, and they built a small house of mud and wattles at Glastonbury. Later on, Joseph fleeing from Palestine settled there and erected a little church. Now in spite of confident assertions to the contrary it must be definitely said that there is neither any early tradition nor any real evidence of this. Tales associated with such places as the 'Jesus well' in Cornwall and 'Paradise' in Somerset are historically worthless. William of Malmesbury (1100), whose statements are the principal source of the stories, can hardly be deemed a reliable witness, writing as he does a thousand years after the events. But the conclusive argument against their truth is the fact that while many Church Fathers speak of the Gospel having spread to Britain – Tertullian, Origen, Eusebius, Jerome, and others – none of them have any knowledge at all of these tales. How could they have possibly missed such sensational news if it were true?

The alleged letter of Augustine (who came to Britain in 597) to Pope Gregory, for which William of Malmesbury is again the only authority, is interesting and may be quoted:

In the western confines of Britain there is a certain royal island of large extent, surrounded by water, abounding in all the beauties of nature and necessaries of life. In it the first neophytes of Catholic law, God beforehand acquainting them, found a church constructed by no human art, but by the hands of Christ himself, for the salvation of his people. The Almighty has made it manifest by many miracles and mysterious visitations that he continues to watch over it as sacred to himself and to Mary, the mother of God.

Even if this letter could be proved genuine, its meaning and implications would remain extremely doubtful, and six hundred years is ample time for the most fantastic tales to grow up and become generally believed. The utmost we can say is that Glastonbury may well be the oldest shrine in Britain, and that it may quite possibly date back to the second century.

Three modern apocrypha may be mentioned. The silent years of the life of Jesus – his boyhood and youth – have always exercised a fascination for many people, and various fictional studies of them have been written, some of great beauty and insight. But in 1911 a German writer, E. E. von der Planitz, published a book entitled *Ein Jugendfreund Jesu* which purported to be a first-century letter from an Egyptian doctor, Benan, to a friend describing a youthful residence of Jesus in Egypt, his friendship with Benan, and later on the latter's arrival at Jerusalem at the time of the crucifixion. This story had some vogue in Germany, but in 1924 it was fully and finally exposed by two scholars, Schmidt and Grapow. The non-publication of any original document was of course fatal to the claim made for the story.

More complicated questions arise in connexion with another book, *The Unknown Life of Jesus Christ*, by Nicholas Notovich. It was published in French in 1895, a number of editions appearing and several English translations. It professed to tell the story of the writer's journey to Tibet and of his discovery there of ancient records regarding Jesus, preserved in a monastery and translated into French for him by one of the monks. These described a visit paid to India by Jesus in his youth, and his preaching in Palestine on his return. His name is rendered as 'Issa' and in various ways the story contradicts the Gospels – the Jews are depicted as favouring him, and Pilate as effecting his downfall and removing his body from the tomb. Several scholars argued convincingly that the whole thing was a fabrication, Albert Schweitzer calling it 'a barefaced swindle and an impudent forgery'. Interest in the matter was, however, reopened in 1926 by the announcement that Professor Roerich of New York had visited this same monastery and acquired certain manuscripts telling this same story; this suggests that there may have been substance in Notovich's story – though not of course in the contents of the document. A possible explanation of the business is that it dates from the thirteenth century, when it is known that Christianity had penetrated into those regions. Buddhist priests, alarmed at the progress of the Gospel, may have adopted certain Christian teachings and ceremonies in an attempt to counteract its influence by stealing its thunder, so to speak. One quotation may be made:

A spy approached Issa saying, Teacher, should we fulfil the will of Caesar or await the approaching deliverance? Issa, recognizing the disguised servant, said, I have not said unto you that you would be delivered, but I have said that the soul immersed in sin would be delivered.

This looks like a garbled paraphrase of the tribute-money story in the Gospels, but there is certainly a sort of insight about it. It may indicate the presence of Gospel manuscripts there at the date mentioned, but of course it does not give any independent evidence or information.

The third book was published in French in 1894, with what was said to be the original Latin text. The editor, Catulle Mendès, stated that it was 'found some years ago in the ancient abbey of St Wolfgang in the Salzkammergut.' The opening words of the document claim St Peter as the author, but in point of fact it is, as Dr M. R. James says, a sentimentalized compilation from various apocryphal Gospels; its late date is proved by the fact that it contains phrases from the Latin version of one of these Gospels which was not made until 1697. He thinks that there is no doubt that the Latin text as well as the French version is really the work of Mendès. A translation into English appeared in 1904, entitled *The Childhood of Christ*, by Henry Copley Greene.

These books are mentioned here because they may so easily mislead uninstructed readers, and because there is always a chance of further 'spurious evidence' of this type being published to the hurt of the unwary. Understanding of the inclination to apocryphalize – if one may coin a word – is an important aspect of the critical faculty.

CHAPTER 20

EPILOGUE – THE SUM OF THE MATTER

———

IN attempting to assess the results of our study we commence with the question of the historicity of Jesus. We have not of course examined in detail what is called 'the Christ-myth theory' – that is outside our scope, and in any case the arguments in refutation of it have settled the matter for most reasonable people; H. G. Wood's excellent little book *Did Christ Really Live?* is a very convincing statement. Our assembling of evidence from pagan, Jewish, and extra-canonical Christian sources, builds up an impressive case for the defence – one point of particular importance being the tacit assumption in all these early writers that Jesus was a historical character; had there been any slightest suspicion to the contrary at that time, the opponents of the Church would have leapt on to it with gusto.

The devastating verdict of Sir James Frazer has already been quoted in this connexion, but we may add the following emphatic statement of Dr T. R. Glover: 'If the ordinary canons of history, used in every other case, hold good in this case, Jesus is undoubtedly an historical person. If he is not an historical person, the only alternative is that there is no such thing as history at all – it is delirium, nothing else; and a rational being would be better employed in the collection of snuff-boxes. And if history is impossible, so is all other knowledge.' Strong words for a Lecturer in Ancient History at the University of Cambridge – but striking and valuable testimony, not lightly to be set aside.

And it is not only his historicity that is confirmed by this extra information that we have gleaned concerning him, but the general aspects of his character – and of the Christian way of life as his followers understood and lived it. It is essentially the same Jesus whom we know from the Gospels that we meet with in the agrapha and other uncanonical matter. There are frequent references to his humility and gentleness, and stress is laid upon such qualities as right and proper for Christian people. We get some glimpses of what we may call the theological or doctrinal Christ, but it is the moral features of his personality which predominate. This confirms our feeling of the tremendous impact that he made on men – the unique impression that he gave of being the way, the truth, and the life. A modern writer has well said of Jesus that he was 'like a meteor streaming in light across the world, whose kindling and enlightening rays could never again be extinguished.' .

We come now to the question whether any fresh knowledge of Jesus has come to us from beyond the Gospels. Leaving the agrapha on one side for the moment, the answer must be – very little. There are one or two slight references of interest, such as those of Justin to the cave of the Nativity and the work Jesus did as a carpenter; there is a striking description of his appearance when he cleansed the Temple, and the statement that at the crucifixion a great stone fell from the gateway and was smashed; and there are a number of elaborations of incidents recorded in the Gospels, such as the use of olive-branches at the Entry, and the introduction of individuals' names into certain stories. Several conversations (including agrapha) have been thought genuine by some scholars – that of Salome and Jesus regarding marriage, and of the brothers of Jesus with him regarding baptism. The account of the resurrection appearance to James, the brother of Jesus, has also often been considered authentic.

More important perhaps than these details are the constant references in the Islamic passages to the teaching of Jesus regarding poverty and wealth, in which it seems quite likely that a true reminiscence is embedded of an aspect of his thought which has been commonly underestimated; and again, the suggestion in the Slavonic Josephus that the political implications of the Gospel were more fully recognized in early days than has been commonly supposed. Both these points may perhaps be felt to be positive contributions to our thought of Jesus and our understanding of his message.

As regards the agrapha generally, I believe that a considerable number of them are worthy of respect and may in all probability have originated from him; whether they have come down to us in the form in which he uttered them is of course another question, though I would say that in not a few cases we probably have his *ipsissima verba*. It would not be difficult to gather some twenty or thirty suitable for inclusion in such an appendix to the Gospels as Dr Rendel Harris once spoke of (see p. 16). Without attempting to do this, I would at least urge that we should not neglect this material, but that it should be made more use of in preaching and teaching than has normally been the case, and that future Lives of Christ should take more cognizance of it than in the past.

It may of course be felt by some scholars that I am too optimistic in my view of these stories and sayings. I have already discussed how difficult it is to test the genuineness of such material, but one further illustration may be given. One of the most generally accepted of these passages is the striking little tale of the man working on the Sabbath (see p. 123). It is found only in the Gospel manuscript known as Codex Bezae, now in the University Library, Cambridge. Now this manuscript was brought to this country in the sixteenth century by Theodore Beza, the famous Protestant scholar. If the vessel in which he sailed across the Channel had foundered with all hands, this saying would never have been known. Surely this suggests that weakness of attestation – survival of a saying in one place only, even one of comparatively late date – can never of itself be proof that it is not genuine. A thousand and one chances may have contributed to destroy evidence of it, as indeed must have been the case with many authentic utterances of Jesus, now irrecoverably lost. We may not like to deal with possibilities rather than with certainties in matters like these, but I submit that we have no option.

Of course the subjective element must enter into this business – everyone must decide for himself regarding the worth of this material. But 'worth' should surely not be interpreted solely in terms of historical authenticity. As I have said earlier, false anecdote may be good history; it may be *ben trovato*, well invented and true to the life and character of the person of whom it is told. To gain currency it must be true in spirit if not in actual fact. And I consider that, though there are many strictly genuine elements amongst the agrapha, there are also many which are valuable in this secondary sense – that they also help us to see Jesus and to understand his meaning and his message for mankind.

For my own part anyhow I feel like one who, turning over forgotten papers in a long-neglected box, has come upon some old and faded photographs of a dear friend; they cannot bear comparison with those lovely portraits of him which we rightly cherish as our most sacred treasures, but they too may have a place in our esteem and in our memory.

INDEX

INDEX

This Index is divided into three parts:

    I. *Ancient books and writers*
    II. *Modern authors*
    III. *Miscellaneous*

Place names are not included, nor Bible books or characters

I

II

III

*Some other Pelican and Penguin books
on allied subjects are described
on the following pages*

The Dead Sea Scrolls

J. M. ALLEGRO

A376

In the early summer of 1947 an Arab shepherd stumbled upon a cave near the Dead Sea containing seven ancient scrolls. They proved to be part of the library of a Jewish monastic community living before and during the time of Christ. Later discoveries produced the remains of hundreds more scrolls from the same source, so that to-day we have an undreamt-of insight into Jewish sectarianism of this all-important period. It is already clear that many of the characteristic ideas of Jewish Christianity were cradled in just such a religious environment.

The study of this exciting new evidence is fast becoming a field of research on its own account, and this book surveys in popular form some of the more important results so far achieved, with a particular orientation towards New Testament studies where, it is now clear, the main interest of these priceless documents must lie.

Christianity and Social Order

WILLIAM TEMPLE

A345

Dr William Temple, whose work earned him the title 'the People's Archbishop', strove throughout his life to rebuild the shattered social teaching of the Church, for he believed that all secular policy should be founded upon theological truth. To this end he devoted much of his preaching and writing. In 1942 he wrote *Christianity and Social Order* for the Penguin Specials. It is not a plea for more political influence for the Church, but a bid to make social questions subject to Christian morality and especially to the doctrine of the dignity and importance of the individual. This book was republished in the Pelican series in the hope that interest in the work of the great archbishop will be revived.

In An Age of Revolution

CYRIL GARBETT

A 368

This book was written by the late Archbishop of York in the conviction that mankind is now in the midst of one of the greatest crises of history. It is due to three causes: the rejection of Christian faith and morals, an uncompromising attack on Western civilization, and the violent social and economic upheavals both in the East and the West.

The first section gives some account of the revolution of the last seventy years, and of the effect it has had on both faith and morals. The second section describes and criticizes some of the alternatives which have gained man's allegiance and which have served for a time as substitutes for Christianity. In the last section the Christian answer to the crisis is given, with some account of the manner in which the Church is adapting its methods of work to changed conditions.

Communism and Christianity

MARTIN D'ARCY

s163

Communism has been called a religion, and in so far as it has a creed which is wholeheartedly believed the name is not unjustified. What the Apostles' Creed is for Christianity, the Communist Manifesto is to its followers, a call to belief and action. Both creeds claim to give an answer to the chief problems which agitate man – his individual and social life, his origin and destiny.

The aim of this book is to compare their answers, to examine their validity, and to see how far they are at variance and where, if at any place, they come together. The writings of Marx are first studied; an account is then given of the development of Communism. Its ideas are examined and then contrasted with the principal tenets of Christian philosophy, which has had a formative influence on the culture of the West and which touches the same concerns and problems as its Communist rival.